OLD PILOTS, BOLD PILOTS

LANDMARKS IN COMMERCIAL AVIATION:
THE TRIUMPHS AND THE DISASTERS

BY

ARCHIE JACKSON

CIRRUS ASSOCIATES

PUBLISHED BY:
Cirrus Associates (S.W.),
Kington Magna,
Gillingham,
Dorset,
SP8 5EW UK.

ISBN 0 951 5598 7 7

PRINTED IN ENGLAND BY:
The Book Factory,
35-37 Queensland Road,
London,
N7 7AH.

PHOTO SCANNING BY:
Castle Graphics Ltd.,
Nunney,
Nr. Frome,
Somerset,
BA11 4LW.

DISTRIBUTOR:
Cirrus Associates (S.W.),
Kington Magna,
Gillingham,
Dorset,
SP8 5EW.

COVER:
From an original painting by Saffron Streat

DEDICATION

For Saffron

ACKNOWLEDGEMENTS

Many of the chapters were first published as separate articles in various aviation magazines, that are acknowledged below by the author. They appear here with only minor alterations due to corrections and updating.

Chapters 1, 4, 7, 12, 16, 17, 18 & 22: *"Aircraft Illustrated."*
Chapters 5, 6, 10 & 15: *"Wingspan."*
Chapter 19: *"Aeroplane Monthly."*
Chapters 3 & 21: *"Air Pictorial."*

CONTENTS

INTRODUCTION   7

PART 1: THE PIONEERS

CHAPTER 1: THE U.K.'S FIRST AIRLINES   13

CHAPTER 2: BRABAZON OF TARA –
THE FIRST ENGLISHMAN
TO FLY AN AEROPLANE   21

CHAPTER 3: HARRY HAWKER –
PILOT AND DESIGNER   27

CHAPTER 4: CHARLES KINGSFORD SMITH –
AUSTRALIA'S FOREMOST AIR PIONEER   33

CHAPTER 5: RAY HINCHLIFFE –
FORGOTTEN AIR PIONEER   41

CHAPTER 6: GORDON OLLEY'S AIR SERVICE   53

CHAPTER 7: ALAN COBHAM –
A LIFETIME OF SERVICE TO AVIATION   59

CHAPTER 8: SIDNEY COTTON –
CONFLICT WITH THE BUREAUCRATS   70

CHAPTER 9: EDWARD HILLMAN –
FROM BUS DRIVER TO AIRLINE BOSS   79

PART 2: THE VENTURERS

CHAPTER 10: THE SOUTH ATLANTIC PIONEERS   87

CHAPTER 11: CAPTAIN GORDON STORE –
FROM PUSS MOTHS TO THE BIG JETS   92

CHAPTER 12: THE LAST GREAT AIR RACE   98

CHAPTER 13: GEORGE WOODS HUMPHERY –
SCAPEGOAT FOR A TROUBLED AIRLINE   106

CHAPTER 14: THE EMPIRE FLYING BOATS
IN WARTIME   118

CHAPTER 15: SKY TRAMPS AND SCAMPS IN THE
POSTWAR AIR CHARTER SCENE   124

CHAPTER 16: SELLING THE SUPER VC.10   132

PART 3: "HOSTAGES TO FATE"

CHAPTER 17: AIRSHIP R.101 –
THE HUMAN FACTOR IN THE DISASTER 141

CHAPTER 18: THE BERLIN AIRLIFT –
A CITY SAVED FROM STARVATION 153

CHAPTER 19: THE AVRO TUDOR –
ONE MAN'S STRUGGLE TO PROVE
ITS WORTH 159

CHAPTER 20: THE HANDLEY PAGE HERMES –
NOBODY'S FAVOURITE AIRLINER 164

CHAPTER 21: THE COMET 1 –
THE WORLD'S FIRST JET AIRLINER 170

CHAPTER 22: THE MUNICH AIR DISASTER –
THE CAUSE DISPUTED 178

CONCLUSION: 186

INTRODUCTION

It used to be said that there were old pilots and bold pilots but that few of the bold pilots survived the inherent dangers of flying to become old pilots. There were no commercial airlines before the first World War and when peace was restored aircraft manufacturers met the demand for civil airliners by converting military machines.

The pilots were young Royal Flying Corps men who in the circumstances of the time must be included in the category of bold pilots. Many had gone into action with fewer than twenty hours in their log books; they were the survivors of a very perilous occupation – aviation. Even without the threat of hostile aircraft in the skies many dangers still prevailed. Wearing leather helmets and goggles, the pilots sat in open cockpits, often soaked by rain, with no provision for heating. Forward visibility was impaired by oil sprayed from the engine onto the windscreen. No protection against airframe icing existed; instrumentation for blind flying was in its infancy, as was any system of wireless communication or the dissemination of weather information.

Pilots were often obliged to fly below the lowest layer of clouds in order to keep a check on their progress along their chosen route. In bad weather this increased the risk of collision with church steeples, tall buildings or rising ground. If the engine failed a landing had to be attempted immediately on any unobstructed field within view. Not surprisingly there were many accidents. Every pilot knew that there were risks involved in aviation. The insurance companies loaded the policies of pilots until the 1950s.

In the early 1920s converted bombers began to be replaced by the new designs of aircraft manufacturers. Enclosed passenger cabins were followed by enclosed cockpits although many pilots preferred to feel the fresh winds on their faces. Airliners powered by two or three engines became available but were not necessarily safer to fly. Some could not maintain altitude with one engine out of action.

In addition to those pilots employed by the airlines a new breed of venturers took to the skies. Some sought sponsors in their attempts to achieve a distance record or a faster time over a lengthy stage. Newspaper proprietors and manufacturers of aviation fuels offered prizes to those who successfully concluded a record-breaking flight.

The first part of this book relates the experiences of some remarkably bold pilots. Best remembered are Lord Brabazon, Sir Alan Cobham, Harry Hawker and Charles Kingsford Smith. Forgotten today is Raymond Hinchliffe who embarked upon a transatlantic flight when his impaired eyesight was about to deprive him of his pilot's licence. Fearful for the future of his wife and children he took out an insurance policy for their benefit. Hinchliffe lost his life over the Atlantic.

The second section of the book introduces the venturers who were active between the two World Wars. The dictionary defines "venturer" as "one who undertakes a trading venture." However the word "venturesome" is more explicit: it means "disposed to take risks, daring, perilous." The South Atlantic Pioneers were Frenchmen and Germans pursuing their national commercial interests. A British pilot, Gordon Store, set a record to South Africa in the company of a young female sponsor. He went on to become a senior Imperial Airways captain and an airline executive. Woods Humphery had been a Royal Flying Corps pilot before becoming the driving force of Imperial Airways. The restrictive constitution of that airline forced him into the role of scapegoat when in 1938 their landplanes were described as "the laughing stock of Europe."

Other venturers such as Jim Mollison and Amy Johnson, Scott and Campbell Black made their living out of attempts to break records and win air races. These venturers must still be classified in the category of bold pilots. Like Lindbergh in his astonishing flight across the Atlantic Ocean to Paris they had to stay awake and sufficiently alert to navigate and land safely after an incredibly long spell at the controls.

After the second World War the dearth of British civil airliners witnessed the reappearance of converted bombers. The government would only release scarce American dollars to enable B.O.A.C. to buy some Lockheed Constellations and maintain a transatlantic service. Venturers such as Freddie Laker and Harold Bamberg bought the converted bombers to operate commercial services on charters and on routes neglected by the airways corporations. Less scrupulous individuals also entered that market; regulations concerning hours on duty by flight crews were often ignored.

The Russian blockade of Berlin resulted in an airlift involving every available transport aircraft. This event prolonged the working life of converted bombers and their operators. The raising of the siege saw many private companies go out of business.

The VC.10 project was a venture by Vickers who, against the usual trend, did not intend to ask the government for financial help. Early in the 1950s B.O.A.C. had a requirement for an airliner that could carry an adequate payload from aerodromes at a high altitude in a tropical climate. Prior to this Vickers had developed a long-range transport for the R.A.F. that had been cancelled shortly before the first flight. On this occasion their design was close to B.O.A.C.'s specifications. The Super VC.10 that emerged delighted the pilots who flew it and the passengers welcomed the smooth ride and quiet cabin. Yet despite the high load factors that were achieved and the popularity the aircraft enjoyed, the operating costs conflicted with the priorities of B.O.A.C.'s accountants and engineers. More important to the latter were the benefits to be obtained from membership of Boeing's spares pool. Sadly the VC.10 was never developed through improved models. Nevertheless it remains the principal long-range transport of the R.A.F.

I have named the last part of this book "Hostages to Fate," aware that this may provoke controversy.

Lord Brabazon of Tara was chairman of the Air Registration Board when the decision to authorise the resumption of Comet 1 services, after the crash at Elba, was taken. He told the House of Lords:

"Of course we offered hostages to fate but I cannot believe that this court or our country will censure us because we ventured . . . "

The story of the R.101 airship disaster a quarter of a century earlier reveals similar heart-searching by responsible individuals when a lengthy delay in the introduction to service of the airship culminated in political pressures to permit Lord Thomson of

Cardington to travel to India for a Commonwealth conference. It was his ambition to be the next Viceroy.

Britain's first two pressurised four-engined long-range airliners both suffered grave disasters. The prototype Hermes crashed, as did the Avro Tudor. An Avro Tudor disappeared without trace en route to Bermuda and the type was grounded for safety checks. No dangerous faults were discovered and passenger flights resumed. One year later another Tudor disappeared without trace over the Western Atlantic. At that stage the airline felt obliged to withdraw the type from service.

The Hermes had an unhappy operating history with B.O.A.C. On two occasions a propeller detached itself during flight and struck the aircraft, causing injuries. B.O.A.C.'s reason for withdrawing it from service was the high operating cost and poor payload. Offered for sale at a bargain price six were bought by Airwork Ltd. Propeller problems continued and there were two crashes. Skyways Ltd bought twelve Hermes from B.O.A.C. and two of these suffered damage from a propeller shedding during flight. The type was flown by its various owners for twelve years. It was never grounded. A series of modifications to eliminate the propeller problem was never totally successful.

In time of war air travellers became hostages to fate. Politically inspired hijackers have often been a threat. During the Berlin airlift the Russians sent up fighters to dive at and fire alongside the transport pilots.

However the Munich Air Disaster was in no way the result of political hostility. The progress of aviation has inevitably revealed dangers that had either been overlooked or inadequately appreciated. The failure of B.E.A.'s Elizabethan to become airborne at Munich destroyed the reputation of the aircraft captain and cost the lives of many on board, but ultimately the investigations revealed the retarding effect of even a thin layer of slush on the ability of aircraft to build up an adequate speed to unstick from the runway.

PART 1

THE PIONEERS

CHAPTER 1

THE U.K.'S FIRST AIRLINES

Seventy-five years ago, as the delegates of the victorious powers of the first World War gathered in Versailles to draw up the peace treaty, various interested parties were already making plans to inaugurate commercial airline services from Britain to Europe.

Aircraft Transport and Travel (A.T. & T.) had been founded in 1916 by George Holt Thomas whose aircraft manufacturing company was building Farman aeroplanes under licence to the French parent company (his chief designer was a certain Geoffrey de Havilland!). Their small military DH.4 and DH.9 machines were swiftly converted for civil use and designated Airco 4 and Airco 9. Gen. Sir Sefton Brancker, formerly of the Royal Flying Corps, was appointed managing director. The largest bombers in the R.A.F. had been built by Sir Frederick Handley Page at the works airfield in Cricklewood. With all war contracts cancelled, he worked with one test pilot and a research assistant to adapt his machines to convey passengers. Handley Page Transport came into being with the appointment of Maj. Woods Humphery as general manager, Maj. H. Brackley as the air superintendent and Lt. Col. Sholto Douglas, who was engaged as chief pilot. Another pilot in their employment was Gordon Olley. All were to achieve distinction in the years to come.

In 1917 the British government had appointed the newspaper magnate Lord Northcliffe to be chairman of a committee to study the development and regulation of post-war civil aviation. Years earlier he had offered a prize of £10,000 to the first airman to fly across the North Atlantic Ocean. In 1919 this was won by Alcock and Whitten-Brown in a Vickers Vimy machine. In some respects other goals were to prove more difficult to achieve. In 1910, at an international conference, Great Britain had not been alone in declaring the air above the United Kingdom and her Empire inviolable. In 1919 only Germany was pressing for the freedom of the skies.

Lord Trenchard, "the father of the R.A.F.," was keen to have a thriving civil aviation sector as a reserve for his own service. On the grounds of strategy and prestige, he urged the government to allocate public money for the development of routes to the Empire. So too did the first Controller General of the Department of Civil Aviation, Gen. Sykes, but Lloyd-George's coalition government was deaf to such advice. However, the Air Ministry took over the responsibility for issuing pilots' licences and certificates of airworthiness for civil aircraft.

Meanwhile, Hounslow was declared to be the required airport for customs clearance for flights entering and leaving England. Its grass field was not easy for pilots to find. One shed bore the word "Customs," another the word "'Douane," while a third shed served as a waiting room. The government set a scale of fees for landings and hangar storage space at those four aerodromes which were designated for civil use. Meteorological information was made available, as was a wireless communication service.

Commercial flying was permitted to commence on 14th July 1919, but for one week only, to coincide with the peace celebrations in France. When a Col. Pilkington read this in the London *"Evening News,"* he rang A.T. & T and chartered an aircraft to fly him to Paris. On a day of torrential rain and low cloud, the pilot, Jerry Shaw, flew out of Hendon with his passenger. In his anxiety to make the first commercial flight he decided not to land at Hounslow and pressed on to Le Bourget. To keep the ground in sight he seldom flew above 200 ft and reached Le Bourget in under three hours. This was a muddy field with as few facilities as Hounslow. Their arrival attracted no attention and avoiding passenger formalities they left the airfield and boarded a tram for the city. The next day they flew back to Hounslow where Shaw incurred the wrath of the Customs officer.

The first commercial flight of a Handley Page Transport was flown by Sholto Douglas that same month. This was also a charter, in a 10-passenger HP. 0/400 to Brussels. The airline's publicity stressed the extra safety provided by two Rolls Royce Eagle engines: in fact the machine would not have been able to maintain altitude if one had failed. In August Handley Page inaugurated a regular service to Paris. The fare was the same as the first-class rail and boat fare and a limousine ran the passengers to and from the airfields – a box lunch was provided on payment of a small charge. That month A.T. & T. also began scheduled services to Paris and had completed 147 flights by November. By then a third challenger had appeared on the route.

Sir Samuel Instone and his brother Theodore were shipowners and coal exporters based in Wales. Initially they bought an aeroplane for business use, but they were soon inspired to found the Instone Air Line which entered the gathering competition in October 1919. Their pilot, Franklyn Barnard, flew a converted Vickers Vimy from Hounslow to Le Bourget.

However, these three British companies were not only competing against each other but also against two French airlines and Holland's K.L.M. Even more troubling was the impossibility of matching the fares of foreign airlines. In Holland and Belgium, subsidies were paid by the state. The Germans, denied military aircraft under the terms of the peace treaty, backed several airlines. The larger towns paid these to use their airports. The French were fearful that a revived Germany would threaten them once more and therefore they continued to retain large military forces and supported their airlines as a reserve for their air force. In the autumn of 1919, a railway strike in Britain gave the three domestic airlines a welcome boost to their dwindling financial reserves through the need for extra services.

Because of the pioneering nature of the new air-travel business, those passengers who were brave enough to fly faced heavily-loaded premiums if they took out life insurance policies. Not only were engine failures commonplace but the weather was a perpetual hazard. Blind flying instruments had not been developed: altimeters could not be relied on and compass needles oscillated wildly except when a steady course was flown in calm conditions.

When HM Customs installed an office at Cricklewood, Handley Page was able to operate to the continent without a stop at Hounslow. But the grass field was so short that pilots considered themselves fortunate to be airborne with a mere 100 yds remaining before they flew over the airfield boundary. Aiming between two hangars, the aircraft passed over Cricklewoood Broadway at about 50 ft – an engine failure at that point would have caused disaster.

In March 1920, Hounslow was replaced as a Customs airport by an area of two grass fields which had formerly contained separate R.A.F. aerodromes, Wallington and Waddon. The landing area was on Waddon, so rough and uneven that aircraft could be lost to sight from the tarmac apron on the Wallington side. A factory and a water tower on the perimeter had to be avoided by arriving and departing pilots. Sheep sometimes found their way into the landing area. As happened at Heathrow later in 1946, a haphazard building programme to handle staff, stores and passengers generated wooden huts of all shapes and sizes. There was not a regular bus service and Waddon railway station was some distance away. The residents of Wallington disassociated themselves from the aerodrome, so it was adopted by Croydon. Thus Croydon Aerodrome really became the birthplace of British civil aviation.

Although the French had begun flights to West Africa and the Germans were cooperating with the Russians in running services to Moscow, Teheran and Peking, any hope that a British airline could develop links to the Empire was a distant dream. In addition to the financial constraints the French and Italians banned over-flights while the Germans blocked the route to Prague.

The government steadfastly declined to offer further help. Winston Churchill told the House of Commons: "Civil aviation must fly by itself. The government cannot possibly hold it up in the air."

It is probable that this attitude mirrored the opinion of many in the country. The public was in no mood to pay taxes for the benefit of well-to-do travellers. The political parties shared a common desire to reduce the high level of taxation which the people had endured throughout the war.

At the end of 1920, A.T. & T. went into liquidation. The Instone Air Line could only fly to Paris when there was a sufficient demand for seats and only Handley Page continued with its regular service. In February 1921 all three companies were forced to cease operations, leaving the French and others to fly into Croydon on their own. Consequently British taxpayers were contributing to the upkeep of aerodromes, wireless and weather services used only by foreign airlines. British aircraft manufacturers also faced a bleak future.

In a letter to *"The Times,"* Sir Sefton Brancker deplored the fact that "Holland, Denmark, Norway and Sweden, with few pilots or aircraft of their own manufacture, could have been supplied by England. The result is that Mr Fokker, designer of the most efficient fighting machine which Germany had produced during the war, is to have the order for the equipment."

Business was not looking good for the fledgling British airlines.

Development of civil aviation in the U.K. was very slow, but a change of heart by the government was prompted by a coal miners' strike. This seemed likely to provoke a further strike by sympathetic railwaymen and transport workers. A 'temporary' subsidy was speedily arranged. Handley Page and Instone resumed services when granted an amount which was intended to guarantee them a profit of 100% on gross receipts. Woods Humphery, who had worked for the defunct A.T. & T., helped to persuade the Daimler-BSA combine to put up sufficient money to found Daimler Airway. The Air Ministry made available some DH.18s which had been intended for A.T. & T. Woods Humphery was appointed general manager and the airline aimed to obtain 1,000 hours flying time by each aircraft annually.

By this time, some machines were fitted with Marconi wireless sets with a reception range of about 50 miles, but it was still the normal practice for pilots to navigate by reference to railway lines. A small number of beacons were installed in England and France to guide pilots, each beacon flashing a distinct sign in Morse code. In southern England, railway stations even had their names painted in white on the roof. But flying under these primitive flight rules was dangerous and in April 1922, sadly, a DH.18 of Daimler collided head-on with a Farman Goliath. It is presumed that both pilots were looking down upon the Abbeville-Beauvais road for lack of forward visibility on a foggy day.

These were difficult times for the fledgling airlines and matters were not helped by a severe depression in 1922. However, the situation was soon to change. Sir Sefton Brancker was appointed Director of Civil Aviation and he recommended the creation of one national airline to compete against the Europeans.

At the time, the numbers employed by the three British airlines were derisory when compared to the growing foreign carriers. There were only 13 pilots and 117 other employees. Daimler Airway employed four pilots and possessed two aeroplanes, and became the first airline to engage a steward. He wore a bow tie, a stiff white collar and monkey jacket and was probably very cold as the DH.34 in which he flew was unheated and the passengers invariably wore their overcoats. Meanwhile Instone Airline dressed its pilots in a nautical blue uniform, a fashion that was subsequently copied by most other airlines.

In 1923 the Secretary of State for Air was, for the first time. a member of the Cabinet. He was Sir Samuel Hoare, the first minister to fly on official business, and he was keen to see the development of air routes throughout the Empire. He shared Sir Sefton Brancker's views and proposed the creation of one monopoly company, run on commercial lines with private shareholders – but provided with a total subsidy of an agreed amount spread over 10 years. Among the representatives of the existing airline managements, there should be two government-appointed directors on the Board. Sir Samuel's choice as chairman was Sir Eric Geddes.

Some time passed for all the arrangements to be worked out and Woods Humphery was appointed General Manager with a seat on the board. The name Imperial Airways was adopted and the airline was declared to be the "chosen instrument of the government." The airlines so taken over were Handley Page Transport, Instone Air Line, Daimler Airway and British Marine Air Navigation Co.

Among the terms of the agreement was the condition that the aircraft operated should be of British manufacture. The new company faced the immediate problem of incorporating the staff of the three airlines whom they wished to employ and a motley collection of aeroplanes.

The first Labour government in British history had come to power and Sir Eric Geddes may have wondered whether his new political masters would permit Imperial Airways to function as a commercial monopoly supported by public funds. At any rate the Board's delay in offering contracts to the pilots caused widespread apprehension that the salaries on offer would be less than those previously paid. These had ranged from £827 to £1,000. A further grievance was the appointment of Woods Humphery as general manager. Those who had served under him in Handley Page Transport and in Daimler Airway alleged that he had put pressure on them to fly in bad weather and in defective aircraft in circumstances which they judged to be hazardous.

In March 1924, 16 pilots were offered contracts at £100 a year, plus two pence per mile flown; the contract could be cancelled at one day's notice. The pilots unanimously refused this offer, demanding a higher salary with flying pay based on time in the air, not mileage. For several weeks there was a stalemate. No flying could be undertaken but the company serviced those of the aircraft which it had decided to operate. The pilots formed a union and sent a delegation to the new Secretary of State for Air, Lord Thomson.

The dispute became bitter. Imperial Airways asked the Air Ministry to release RAF pilots to fly their services. Woods Humphery served a writ against the pilots' union, alleging libel. Sir Samuel Instone made the sensible suggestion than an air superintendent be appointed, someone whose reputation was respected by the pilots and upon whom they could depend to represent their views to the Board. This appointment was filled by Maj. Brackley who had left Handley Page Transport in 1921 to advise the Japanese on the formation of a naval air arm. During the war, he had been awarded the DSO and DFC and subsequently had unsuccessfully attempted to make an Atlantic crossing and the first flight to South Africa.

The salary scale was ultimately fixed at a maximum of £880 a year. Among the 18 pilots engaged, Franklyn Barnard was appointed chief pilot. Only 13 aircraft were serviceable and these included two amphibian Sea Eagles that had belonged to the British Marine Air Navigation Company which had operated to the Channel Islands. None of the aircraft had any heating or insulation against the noise. Seating comprised wicker chairs and a few possessed a lavatory. The Handley Page W.8B, which was the first postwar airliner, contained the greatest number of seats.

Imperial Airways was finally able to begin its services on 26th April 1924. Within a few months there were flights to Paris, Brussels, Amsterdam, Ostend, Cologne, Hanover, Berlin, Zurich and Basle. Woods Humphery remained at the helm until 1938 when he was forced to resign. This followed an unpublished report to the government by a select committee, instituted to investigate the management of the airline. It was widely accepted that he had been made the scapegoat for an unworkable compromise in the airline's original constitution.

Maj. Brackley remained as air superintendent until the airline was reorganised as B.O.A.C. in 1939. He had found it difficult to represent the pilots whilst being regarded by the management as one of themselves. Sir Sefton Brancker and Lord Thomson both lost their lives in the crash of the airship R.101 at Beauvais en route to India in 1930. Franklyn Barnard was killed flying a private aeroplane in preparation for the King's Cup Air Race which he had earlier won in 1922. But from these turbulent beginnings, civil aviation in the U.K. as we know it today was born.

CHAPTER 2

BRABAZON OF TARA

THE FIRST ENGLISHMAN TO FLY AN AEROPLANE

John Moore-Brabazon, born in 1884, studied engineering at Cambridge University and spent the vacations as an unpaid mechanic to the pioneer of motor cars, Charles Rolls. Motoring was his first love and on leaving university he became an apprentice at the Darracq works in Paris, graduating as an international racing driver. Both young men were interested in aviation and were members of the Aero Club. Founded in 1901, this was initially concerned with ballooning, but was renamed the Royal Aero Club in 1910.

In 1908 Wilbur Wright brought his aeroplane to Europe and prepared to win the Michelin Cup which was to be awarded for the longest duration flight over a closed circuit. He won this on the last day of the year. He had only two serious competitors. One, Henry Farman, made several unsuccessful attempts before abandoning the contest. The other was Moore-Brabazon. He had acquired a Voisin aeroplane and taught himself to fly it but he had not mastered the art of making turns, nor was he able to accomplish this until January 1909.

In England at that time would-be pilots were subjected to ridicule. Moore-Brabazon urged them to follow his example and emigrate to France. Several did so and later won international acclaim. The first British Aero Show was held in May and he exhibited his Voisin among ten other machines. Later he took it to the Aero Club's aerodrome on the Isle of Sheppey where the Short Brothers had a workshop. There he carried out a flight lasting one minute before he crashed. Oswald Short rushed to his assistance, relieved to find him alive.

"You will have to build me another aircraft," he was told.

Moore-Brabazon abandoned his Voisin and applied himself to the production of an all-British aeroplane. The *"Daily Mail"* was offering a prize of £1,000 to the first Englishman to fly one mile. Short Bros began to construct a machine to his order. It was in fact a copy of a Wright aeroplane for the construction of which Short Bros held the licence. Late in October he succeeded in winning the prize a few days before S.F. Cody and Charles Rolls also met the conditions. Short Bros subsequently claimed that with this achievement they had founded the aircraft industry in the British Isles.

In March 1910 Moore-Brabazon was awarded Pilot's Certificate No.1 by the Royal Aero Club. He celebrated with a flight of over three miles carrying a small pig as passenger to disprove the old proverb. Nine months later he was present at an airshow in Bournemouth when his friend Charles Rolls, after a violent manoeuvre, was thrown out of his aeroplane and killed.

Moore-Brabazon was persuaded by his wife to give up flying and he remained on the ground until 1914 when he volunteered for the Royal Flying Corps. He served on the Western Front, specialising in aerial reconnaissance and photography. He reached the rank of Lieutenant Colonel, was awarded the Military Cross and was three times mentioned in despatches.

In 1918 he was elected to the House of Commons as a Conservative. He retained his interest in aviation and was appointed President of the Royal Aeronautical Society in 1935. He was far better qualified than most MPs to add his voice to debates on the state of the Royal Air Force and Imperial Airways. In 1935 the knowledge that the German air force already exceeded in numbers of aeroplanes the strength of the R.A.F. led to the British government giving first priority to the production of military aircraft. This policy made it impossible for Imperial Airways to replace their old landplanes with modern machines because their constitution prohibited the purchase of foreign equipment.

For this and other reasons Imperial Airways became a target for growing dissatisfaction, their landplanes being described as "the laughing stock of Europe." Moore-Brabazon seconded the motion of Robert Perkins who demanded a public enquiry to compel the Air Ministry to take some action. He accused the Air Ministry of neglecting research. In the United States, so Moore-Brabazon told the House, civil aircraft manufacturers competed with one another and the result was the introduction of variable-pitch propellers, flaps and retractable undercarriages. They had transformed civil aviation, adding 100 mph to its speed.

Speaking of civil aviation in a general sense he declared: "It is far too dangerous. Accidents are not reported in the newspapers because they no longer have news value."

When Winston Churchill replaced Neville Chamberlain as Prime Minister in May 1940 he appointed Moore-Brabazon as Minister of Transport. Seven months later he was moved to become Minister of Aviation Production in succession to Lord Beaverbrook. The latter had the foresight to propose the formation of a special committee to recommend what types of civil transport aircraft should be developed for use after the war. This was a very wise proposal because the national airline, now renamed the British Overseas Airways Corporation, had already been obliged to fly converted military machines. B.O.A.C. was to end the war with few genuine airliners of British manufacture and nothing to compete with the new pressurised Douglas DC-6 or Lockheed Constellation.

In 1942 Moore-Brabazon was granted a peerage and entered the House of Lords as the first Baron Brabazon of Tara. Churchill appointed him chairman of the new committee. The chief designers invited to the first meeting in December 1942 did not include most of those who had experience of civil aircraft. The Bristol Aeroplane Company was not invited, but their technical director heard about it and visited B.O.A.C. to discuss their ideas on a long-range aircraft capable of flying non-stop across the North Atlantic. At the following meeting Bristol was represented. The Committee was informed that their design for a very large aircraft could provide the basis for a long-range airliner. In fact this design had originally been for a bomber and had been rejected.

In August 1943 Brabazon reformed his Committee. Geoffrey de Havilland represented the manufacturing industry and Campbell Orde of B.O.A.C. the airlines. There were two civil servants, Ralph Sorley and William Hildred. Sorley had earlier won the argument to equip the Spitfire with eight guns. It was not the Committee's job to produce designs and it was apparent to Brabazon that the continuing development of more powerful engines would rapidly make obsolete any designs that his Committee chose to recommend. There was a lack of commercial input and no one could produce capital costs, nor operating costs, for a specific number of any type of aircraft. He realised that not every type that they did recommend for production would turn out to be successful. To ensure against failure two competitive designs and two competitive prototypes should be produced of each design.

Initially the Bristol Aeroplane Company was given an order for two prototypes with the promise of an order for production aircraft to follow. The name "Brabazon" was assigned to the type and the number 167. By March 1946, with the war over, construction was in progress and a contract awarded for four Brabazons, the first to fly by April 1947. Inevitably this schedule proved too optimistic and it was September 1949 before the first test flight. No decision had been taken over the choice of engines for the final production line. Meanwhile the prototype was fitted with eight Bristol Centaurus piston engines in pairs, each linked to a contra-rotating propeller.

In 1950 the last two production aircraft were cancelled but the second prototype was fitted with Bristol Proteus turboprops. Unfortunately, even at low power, this engine was failing its compressor blades, turbines blades, bearings and many other parts. By 1952 costs had risen alarmingly whilst Campbell Orde of B.O.A.C. had shown no enthusiasm for the project. Bristol's smaller turboprop aircraft, the Britannia, looked likely to prove more satisfactory and de Havilland's Comet 1 had already gone into passenger service. The Brabazon was abandoned.

During the war Great Britain had led the world in pure jet propulsion systems and the intention of Lord Brabazon was to leapfrog current technology and establish a commanding lead with a generation of pure-jet airliners. Both B.O.A.C. and de Havilland cooperated enthusiastically and the Air Ministry had placed an order for 24 Comet 1s. Introduced into service in May 1952 this airliner attracted great acclaim and foreign orders followed. After the first dramatic crash off Elba early in 1954 the airliners were swiftly modified and reintroduced. Then in April another crash occurred and the Comet 1 was grounded and all orders cancelled.

There were complaints that insufficient studies had been conducted as to the cause after the first accident and that a great risk had been taken in allowing the resumption of services so soon.

Lord Brabazon was Chairman of the Air Registration Board and made a robust defence of his decision before the court of enquiry into the disaster.

"We could not delay flying the Comet for ever . . . you and I know the cause of this accident. It is due to the adventurous pioneering spirit of our race. It has been like that in the past; it is like that in the present and I hope it will be like that in the future. Of course we gave hostages to fate but I cannot believe that this court or our country will censure us because we ventured . . . it is metallurgy, not aeronautics, that is in the dock."

The delay before the strengthened Comet 4 was ready to carry passengers across the North Atlantic allowed Boeing to catch up and easily outsell de Havilland with their larger and faster 707. Happily the Vickers Viscount turboprop, which had made its first flight in 1948, enjoyed considerable success. Powered by four Rolls Royce Darts, with British European Airways as the launch customer, it had only one turboprop competitor and a total of 445 were bought by airlines worldwide. The Committee had authorised Armstrong Whitworth to build two prototypes of their Apollo. This was of comparable size and offered much the same range as the Viscount but its Armstrong Siddeley Mamba engine was a failure. By 1952 there was no commercial future for the aircraft.

The desire to provide B.E.A. with an aircraft to rival the Douglas DC-3 resulted in the Vickers Viking, the brainchild of Barnes Wallis. It entered service in September 1946 and eventually 163 were built. The Brabazon Committee's alternative selection was the Airspeed Ambassador, also ordered by B.E.A. Development problems delayed its introduction into service until 1952. Then Airspeed was taken over by de Havilland. Production of the Ambassador was halted in favour of military orders as a consequence of the Korean War.

The Brabazon Committee had made no recommendation regarding flying boats but, as the Saunders Roe Princess (SR.45) has come to be coupled with the Brabazon in the memories of many as the second "white elephant," an explanation of its engines is appropriate. Saunders Roe were keen to build a very large flying boat to be powered by gas turbine engines and provided with a pressurised cabin. The development of the turboprop promised availability of far greater power. In 1947 the design was finalised and the first postwar Ministry of Civil Aviation ordered three aircraft to be operated by B.O.A.C.

Unfortunately the decision to install the same early Proteus engine as in the Brabazon resulted in so many development problems that the first flight was not made until August 1952. Meanwhile B.O.A.C. had abandoned flying boat operations and expressed no interest in flying the Princess. In 1954 all work stopped and they were cocooned. In 1967 they were broken up.

In retrospect the good intentions of the Brabazon Committee did not bear the expected fruit but it must be recalled that the British aircraft industry was required to make up for about ten years of neglect in the production of civil airliners. The R.A.F. had suffered too, entering the war without a single military transport other than the aged Harrow which was obsolete at the time of its delivery. It was also a tragedy that the Brabazon and Princess were both supplied with the Proteus engine, one of the most inefficient gas turbine power plants ever devised.

Lord Brabazon's autobiography was published in 1956. He concluded the account of his political life with the statement that "anything more miserable or harder work, with less thanks, than being a Minister in wartime I don't know."

There is no word about his subsequent work as Chairman of the Special Committee. One can only surmise that despite his best efforts the results were a considerable disappointment to him.

CHAPTER 3

HARRY HAWKER

PILOT AND DESIGNER

Today an aircraft designer is one member of a highly-qualified team provided with computers, wind tunnels and all the advantages of modern science. All the more remarkable therefore that when Thomas Sopwith, a pioneer British airman, became interested in building aircraft he came to depend on two men with very little education indeed.

Fred Sigrist had originally been engaged to look after the engine on Sopwith's yacht but showed himself to be adept at keeping his employer's aeroplane airworthy. After Sopwith had opened a school of aviation at Brooklands, with himself as chief instructor, he decided to enter a new field, aeronautical design. Sigrist developed a talent in that direction also. By that time Sopwith had also engaged the services of a true genius, Harry Hawker.

Hawker was born in Victoria, Australia, and had left school at the age of 12. He inherited from his blacksmith father a mechanical aptitude and became an expert with engines. He was earning £200 a year looking after a fleet of motor cars when he saw an aeroplane for the first time, a Blériot that had been brought to Australia. This inspired him to emigrate to England, where he arrived in 1911. Lacking any recognised qualifications he was obliged to accept very poorly-paid work but he progressed from motor car engines to the Daimler Aero Engine works. Then he saw an advertisement placed by Sopwith for a mechanic. Sigrist engaged him.

By working 15 hours a day and seven days a week Hawker saved enough money to pay his employer for flying lessons. He proved so proficient that he was entrusted with the first air tests of the Sopwith-Wright in 1912. In October of that year he remained aloft for 8 hours 23 minutes before landing in darkness. He had achieved a new British duration record. Sopwith thereupon gave up serious flying in order to devote himself to management. In 1913

Hawker demonstrated the new Sopwith Tractor aircraft to the Admiralty and Army, both of which placed orders. Following this Sopwith observed with astonishment and delight the success of Hawker and Sigrist in designing and producing the new Tabloid aircraft. It was their custom to make rough sketches of their ideas, sometimes in chalk on the factory floor.

As winter set in at the end of 1913 Hawker was allowed to transport a Tabloid to Australia where he made his first flight in January. This aircraft was the fastest and most manoeuvrable seen in that continent up to that time. Hawker was invited by the Governor General to demonstrate it to him and did so after landing on the lawn of Government House. He made many flights carrying passengers at £20 a time and gave an exhibition before 20,000 spectators on Sydney's racecourse. This tour was self-financing but also gave Hawker an opportunity to introduce improvements to the design that he was able to incorporate on his return to England.

Going ashore at Tilbury Docks he made straight for Brooklands and tried out a new 100 hp Tabloid the same afternoon. In June he attempted to loop the loop from only 1,000 feet. He completed the loop but the aircraft spun down into a tall tree, then fell vertically, dislodging several boughs. Hawker walked away unhurt. That early summer of 1914 a seaplane version of the Tabloid won the Schneider trophy, raising the speed record to 92 mph.

When the war broke out in August both the Army and the Admiralty urgently required aircraft, the former to be sent to the Western Front and the latter to counter the use of Zeppelins by the Germans; but only a few Tabloids and Tractors were immediately available. Sopwith enlarged his design team in order to get prototypes built as soon as possible with any kind of drawings. Thus a newcomer, Herbert Smith, designed the 1½ Strutter, the Dolphin, Snipe and Salamander. There was friction between Smith and Hawker's team, subtly encouraged by Sopwith, to produce the best results. The two designers were often at loggerheads and had little time for each other. Both were intolerant if thwarted.

By the end of 1914 no serviceable Sopwith aircraft remained in France but some of their seaplanes had been taken aboard HMS "Ark Royal." This was before the introduction of a landing deck. The seaplanes had to be winched over the side on to the ocean. In choppy weather when take-off power was required the floats often broke away.

Early in 1916 Hawker was testing three new landplanes. Designed by Herbert Smith the Strutter was equipped with a fixed Vickers gun that fired through the arc of the propeller. The German Fokkers already had this facility and were using it to deadly effect. Both the Royal Flying Corps and Royal Naval Air Service were pressing for deliveries of the Strutter, obliging Sopwith to subcontract construction to other manufacturers such as Fairey Aviation. Another Sopwith machine was a triplane. Hawker was so impressed with its handling qualities that he looped it three times on his initial test. The triplane was ordered by the R.N.A.S. for home defence. The third aircraft was the single-seat Sopwith Pup which entered squadron service early in 1917.

Pilots liked the Pup, finding it easy to handle and free of vices. It could turn inside any German fighter. The Pup was equipped with a French engine, a Le Rhône. During the early part of the war British warplanes were usually provided with foreign engines, notably the Clerget and Hispano Suiza. Later on the Bentley engine was fitted to the Sopwith Snipe and Salamander.

In April 1917 King George V visited Brooklands to observe a demonstration by Hawker of the Sopwith Camel and subsequently complimented the pilot. In squadron service this aircraft got a bad name for its tendency to spin. It was sensitive in responding to the controls, the nose rising in a turn to port and dropping in a turn to starboard. Too tight a turn caused the Camel to go into a spin without warning. The answer was to centralise the controls and push forward the stick but sufficient altitude was needed for recovery to take place. Camels came to be used for ground strafing and could carry four small bombs. They accounted for a record total of 1,294 enemy aircraft.

Hawker had on several occasions established new altitude records, on the last occasion to 24,408 feet. It was his conviction that a Sopwith aircraft would always out-climb a German but never out-dive him. "Always climb" was his advice. Many prototypes were under development at Brooklands in 1917 and Hawker could not be spared to test-fly ordinary production models. If he reported to Sopwith that he was satisfied with a prototype it was handed over to a service pilot for testing at Martlesham Heath. One such was the Snipe, a development of the Camel with a Bentley engine. Pilots' reports were so favourable that orders for 1,700 were received. It proved to be the most sophisticated night-fighter of the war years.

With the return of peace all orders for warplanes ceased. Sopwith asked a friend in the city to wind up the company in a voluntary liquidation. When he was told that it would take two years to do this he came to an agreement with Hawker, Sigrist and one other to build motor cycles. Each of the four put up £5,000 and Sopwith agreed that the firm should take the name Harry Hawker Engineering. Fred Sigrist became managing director.

Before the war Lord Northcliffe, owner of the *"Daily Mail,"* had offered a prize of £10,000 for the first non-stop crossing of the Atlantic ocean. Sopwith was determined to compete and expressed the opinion that the war had allowed aircraft to be developed to the point that more than one current type was capable of a successful crossing. Hawker was the obvious choice of pilot and participated in the conversion of Sopwith's B.1 bomber, which was fitted with a 360 hp Rolls Royce engine. Hawker's choice as navigator was Lieut. Commander Mackenzie-Grieve whom he had met when he had been involved in deck-landing trials. The Air Ministry provided a wireless transmitter and a wind-driven generator was fitted on the side of the fuselage to provide power. At Hawker's suggestion the undercarriage was designed to be jettisoned after take-off to reduce drag. A boat was built in as part of the fuselage decking. The aircraft was given the name *"Atlantic."*

A ground crew accompanied by Fred Sigrist sailed over to Newfoundland to choose a site for take-off and a log shed was built. Hawker and his navigator left for America in March 1919 with an engine expert from Rolls Royce and a cameraman. The aircraft was carried in the hold of their ship. Completing the journey by rail to St. John's it was swiftly erected but there was plenty of snow on the ground and it was necessary to wait for better weather. Other competitors arrived and a team with a Martinsyde aeroplane were staying in the same hotel.

On May 18th at 3.40 pm, Newfoundland time, Hawker took of in *"Atlantic"* and jettisoned the undercarriage. Even before he reached 1,200 feet he became aware that the temperature of the water in the radiator was steadily rising. He guessed that the water was not circulating due to an obstruction in the pipes. Shutting down the engine he dived down to 900 feet before restarting it. This was only temporarily effective. Hawker throttled back to prevent the water boiling. Diving once more he was unable to restart the engine and prepared to ditch.

When "Atlantic" was only ten feet above the water, Grieve, who had been frantically priming the engine, succeeded in getting it to start. There was by now no point in attempting to continue their long flight. Hawker altered course to the south towards the shipping lanes. Soon after dawn in breaks in the mist he glimpsed a small steamer. This was the Danish vessel "Mary" bound for Denmark. They circled the ship firing distress signals, and then Hawker ditched "Atlantic" about a mile ahead of its course. At first it floated well but 40 minutes passed before the boat from "Mary" picked them up.

The ship did not have wireless. As the days passed with no reported sighting all hope for the men's safety was given up. The King sent Mrs Hawker a message expressing his deep sorrow at her tragic loss. When the Danish ship came into the sight of the Buff of Lewis semaphore was employed to convey the news of their rescue. The Admiralty ordered H.M.S. "Woolston" to intercept and the two airmen were transferred to H.M.S. "Revenge" at Scapa Flow. Some time later a ship sailing from Montreal to Danzig sighted the tail of "Atlantic" sticking out of the ocean. The wreckage was winched aboard and taken to Falmouth. Later it was sent to London. The undercarriage, jettisoned on take-off, was also found and removed to a museum in St. John's.

Sadly Hawker did not live long enough to enjoy the full fruits of the new engineering enterprise that bore his name. He was testing a Nieuport Goshawk single-seat racing biplane a few days before the Aerial Derby of 1921. The aircraft crashed and caught fire. Hawker was killed instantly. At the inquest it was revealed that he had a tubercular spine and would have had only a short time to live.

Nevertheless the Hawker name has endured through Hawker Aircraft Ltd to the Hawker Siddeley Aircraft Company and many of their products, such as the Hawker Hurricane, the Hunter and the Harrier, have never been forgotten.

"The Times" remembered him thus:

"Mr Harry Hawker, the pioneer Atlantic airman, and the hero of numerous adventures and hairbreadth escapes, both in the air and on land, met with a tragic death last night between Hendon and Edgware. He was testing a Nieuport machine preparatory to taking part in the Aerial Derby on Saturday.

When over Hale Farm, at a considerable altitude, estimated at about 7,000 feet, flames were seen to shoot from the engine. An eyewitness says Hawker shut off the engine and side-slipped, apparently to put out the flames, but almost immediately the machine nose-dived, turning over several times during its fall, and finally crashed in an open field at Burnt Oak.

Hawker fell clear of the machine, and a doctor and several policemen rushed to the scene. Though he was breathing, he died shortly afterwards without regaining consciousness. The body bore marks of burning, and one leg was fractured.

Major D.R. Verey, of Edgware, stated that the machine was returning to Hendon when it began to dive. When it had dropped from a height of about 7,000 feet to about 2,000 feet it started to spin. Major Verey heard the machine strike the ground with a sound he described as resembling that of a shell falling in the distance. It was still in flames, and set fire to the grass round about.

Mr Hawker was one of our most daring aviators, and his career was marked with thrilling adventures and hairbreadth escapes . . . "

CHAPTER 4

CHARLES KINGSFORD SMITH

AUSTRALIA'S FOREMOST AIR PIONEER

The days when pilots vied with one another to set new records over great distances across oceans and deserts have long since gone. Nor do today's airlines claim to operate a faster service than their competitors over identical distances. The volume of air traffic on busy routes, together with the need to fly at an economical cruising speed, combine to ensure that the airline captain remains a safe distance behind the aircraft preceding his own on the same airway.

The skies were not crowded with aeroplanes in 1919 when a 22-year-old Australian, Captain Charles Kingsford Smith, completed his service in the Royal Flying Corps. Awarded the Military Cross for his bravery in action he was determined to make a career in aviation. Whilst fledgling airlines were carrying a few passengers in converted bombers the most adventurous pilots were being attracted to the prizes being offered for record making flights. Alcock and Whitten-Brown had won Lord Northcliffe's prize of £10,000 for the first crossing of the North Atlantic. The Australian government was offering the same sum to the first men to fly from England to the Dominion.

This was the opportunity Kingsford Smith was seeking. He bought a war-surplus Blackburn Kangaroo and declared his intention to enter the contest. It was the first of many frustrations that he had to endure when the Australian government rejected him as lacking in experience. The prize was won by two fellow countrymen, the brothers Ross and Keith Smith, flying a Vimy. To earn a living he exchanged his Blackburn for a DH.6 and offered joyrides. There was so little profit in this that he set off for Hollywood to engage in stunt flying for the motion picture industry. The exploits demanded of the pilots were so dangerous that after witnessing several fatal accidents Kingsford Smith returned to Australia in 1921.

He found work with a flying circus, Diggers Aviation, but was dismissed after damaging an aircraft in an attempt to take off with a flat tyre. He was happier with West Australian Airways which operated six Bristol Tourers; these were converted Bristol F.2 fighters. Kingsford Smith remained with W.A.A. until 1926, becoming their chief pilot.

During this time he formed a friendship with another pilot, Charles Ulm, whose acumen in business affairs, a talent he himself conspicuously lacked, was crucial to their future partnership. The two men were keen to raise enough money to form an airline that would link the state capitals with New Zealand. To attract publicity and financial help they, together with another pilot, Keith Anderson, bought two Bristol Tourers. Kingsford Smith and Ulm circumnavigated Australia, completing the journey in ten days. This achievement attracted the publicity that they had hoped for and provided an opportunity to announce their intention to make the first flight across the Pacific ocean from California to Australia.

The Dominion government showed no interest but under pressure from the ex-servicemen's league the government of New South Wales and *"The Sun"* newspaper offered limited financial support. The three pilots sailed to San Francisco, their first task being to buy an aircraft capable of flying the immense distance across the ocean. The Arctic explorer, Sir Hubert Wilkins, offered them a trimotor Fokker but this lacked engines and instrumentation. Moreover, the price demanded was beyond their slender resources. Then a Melbourne businessman made them a gift of £1,500, but reluctantly, not wishing his name to be associated with a venture that could cost the pilots their lives.

At the time a wealthy pineapple canner had sponsored an air race to Hawaii. This had attracted a number of individuals foolhardy enough to attempt the 2,100 miles flight in single-engined machines. Seven pilots including a woman had lost their lives and the fickle public were temporarily disenchanted by such stunts. The government of New South Wales lost patience over the delay and withdrew its support. With the airmen's funds almost exhausted Keith Anderson decided to return home. The venture seemed doomed, but then an American millionaire, Captain

Hancock, offered to buy the Fokker as his own for the use of Kingsford Smith and Ulm.

It remained necessary to convince the Admiral responsible for airfield and communication facilities that the flight had a reasonable chance of success. He was won over when he was told that the Fokker would be powered by three new Wright Whirlwind engines and that a navigator and wireless operator, both Americans, would accompany the two pilots.

Kingsford Smith and Ulm named their aircraft *"Southern Cross."* A sour note was introduced by an Australian aircraft designer who complained that many of their compatriots had died from the bullets fired by Fokker aircraft; a British machine should have been chosen. On 31st May 1928 *"Southern Cross"* flew out of Oakland airport and landed at Honolulu 27 hours later. So much fuel had to be loaded for the next stage to Fiji that the take-off was made from a beach. After 33 hours they put down at Suva, the first aircraft ever to land on the Fiji group of islands. They reached Brisbane on 9th June. Their total flying time was 83 hours and 11 minutes.

At various times during this first-ever crossing of the Pacific Ocean the weather had been very bad. The two pilots sat in an open cockpit behind a windscreen smeared with oil from the forward engine. Often they were numb with the cold or soaked by rain. The Fokker of the *"Southern Cross"* type was not an easy aircraft to handle, the controls heavy, directional control difficult due to the small fin and rudder, the large wing section and slab-sided fuselage.

The success of the enterprise brought Kingsford Smith and Ulm a grant of £5,000 from the Dominion government and other subscribers brought the total to £20,000. In a gracious gesture the two airmen gave £1,000 of the prize money to Keith Anderson. Captain Hancock generously made a gift of *"Southern Cross"* to the record-makers. The Australian press found it convenient to contract Kingsford Smith's name to "Smithy" and this was how he continued to be known.

In their determination to gain further publicity and financial support for their proposed airline, Australian National Airlines, the two airmen flew *"Southern Cross"* on the first non-stop flight from

Melbourne to Perth in 10 hours on 8th August 1928. The following month they made the first crossing of the Tasman Sea, flying from Sydney to Christchurch, New Zealand. It was a great disappointment that the New Zealand government was reluctant to award operating rights to a company utilising Fokkers, rather than a British aircraft. They would have been willing to have the Sikorsky flying boat built under licence in Britain but these would not have been delivered for several years.

Today "Imperial preference" is a long-forgotten commercial practice. Indeed the recent Labour government of Australia intended to sever the constitutional link with the monarchy. At that time Australians were proud to call themselves British subjects by birth, a statement recorded in their passports. There was not then a British airliner suitable for the long distances separating Australian cities. For this reason Kingsford Smith and Ulm arranged for A.V. Roe to build five Fokker trimotors under licence. They would be imported into Australia free of the tax that would have been imposed on foreign-manufactured aircraft.

In March 1929 Kingsford Smith and Ulm set off in *"Southern Cross"* for England to collect their new aircraft and to engage qualified flight crew and engineers. It was one of the defects of the Fokker that it was unsuited to good wireless reception. En route to Wyndham they failed to receive a report that heavy rain had made the airfield unusable. Entering an area of severe storms that made accurate flying by compass impossible they became lost and eventually put down, their aircraft undamaged, on a mudflat 150 miles west of Wyndham.

Among those who took part in the search for *"Southern Cross"* was Keith Anderson. He too made a forced landing but died of thirst before his aircraft was spotted. Twelve days into the original search the Fokker was found and its crew rescued. This event brought to Kingsford Smith publicity of quite the wrong kind. Before the start of the flight Ulm had contracted to write an account of their journey for a newspaper. His diary of the relevant period, when published, was interpreted by rival newspapers to indicate a deliberate intention to get "lost" in order to attract publicity. By linking the death of Keith Anderson to such a plan Kingsford Smith's detractors seized the opportunity to depict him as self-seeking and ruthless in his ambitions. On his return to Sydney a hostile crowd booed and hissed him.

Late in June he and Ulm set off for England once more, setting a new record of under 13 days. The five Fokkers that had been ordered were delivered before the end of the year and A.N.A. inaugurated a service between Sydney and Brisbane on 1st January 1930. Two of the pilots who had been engaged were former R.A.F. officers whose names were to become well-known. In the future Jim Mollison and C.W.A. Scott both broke long-distance records set by their employer.

Kingsford Smith was convinced that such flights kept his name and organisation in the minds of the Australian government and public. He needed their support to stay in business. Leaving Ulm in Australia to run the business he arranged to fly *"Southern Cross"* across the North Atlantic with a co-pilot provided by K.L.M. They left Croydon on the 1st June 1930 but remained in Dublin until the 24th awaiting a forecast of favourable weather. The urge to fly westward across the ocean had already cost a number of lives including those of two experienced Imperial Airways pilots, Minchin and Hinchliffe. The prevailing westerly winds severely reduced speed whilst the frontal systems presented the hazards of ice formation on the wings.

Dublin's Baldonnel airfield was very small and *"Southern Cross"* was carrying the maximum possible fuel. Kingsford Smith decided to take off from the beach at Portmarnock. Very many hours later the navigator identified the Avalon Peninsula through a break in the fog over the Newfoundland Banks. They landed at the Harbour Grace airfield after a flight of 31½ hours. When they reached New York they were treated to a ticker-tape reception and a personal welcome from President Hoover. They flew on in easy stages to Chicago, Salt Lake City and Oakland, California, thereby completing the circumnavigation of the world.

After returning to England Kingsford Smith bought an Avro Avian open-cockpit biplane powered by one Gipsy engine. In this machine he set out in October to break Bert Hinkler's record for a solo flight to Australia. He was successful and reached Darwin in just under 10 days, making 10 stops over the distance of 10,070 miles. The Australian government rewarded him with the rank of honorary air commodore in the R.A.A.F.

It was a source of frustration and no little bitterness to Kingsford Smith that while these flights brought good publicity, adulation and many invitations to speak at civic functions, very little in the way of financial support was forthcoming. When one of A.N.A.'s Fokkers disappeared in March 1931 on a flight from Sydney to Melbourne the enquiry revealed that the route was not provided with radio beacons or an adequate system of air-to-ground communications. It was implied that A.N.A. bore the responsibility for providing these and the licence to operate the route was withdrawn. The search for the missing airliner (only found in the Snowy Mountains 27 years later) cost A.N.A. £10,000 and was to oblige Kingsford Smith to put the company into voluntary liquidation.

But before that happened he had a part to play in the experimental air mail service introduced between England and the Dominion. The plan was for Imperial Airways to carry the mail in Armstrong Whitworth Argosy airliners to Darwin. Qantas would carry it on to Brisbane and A.N.A. would fly it out to Sydney and Melbourne. The first Argosy, running short of fuel, crash-landed at Koepang on Timor Island. Kingsford Smith flew "Southern Cross" to Koepang to recover the mail and pick up the pilot. He also took part in subsequent air mail trials.

In May 1931 the worldwide economic depression hit Australia and the air mail flights were disrupted by crashes on inadequate airfields. With his airline forced to cease operations Kingsford Smith had to offer joyrides in "Southern Cross" to earn a living. This brought criticism that it was not a fitting occupation for an air commodore. But far more criticism fell upon him when he failed to compete in the celebrated air race between Mildenhall in England and Melbourne, to mark the centenary of that city's foundation.

Kingsford Smith had flown out of Sydney in "Southern Cross" to take part in this race when the cowling of one of the engines developed splits in a dozen places. He had no choice but to turn back for repairs and he found that insufficient time would remain for the aircraft to be present at Mildenhall for the start of the race. His critics were quick to accuse him of deliberately avoiding the contest against other experienced record-breakers such as Mollison or C.W.A. Scott. The latter was the eventual winner, in company with Campbell Black. It was said that he would compete only when he felt certain of victory. Such taunts caused him to write in his autobiography: "A nation's hero may often become a nation's whipping-boy overnight."

It was some compensation that the incoming Liberal government recommended Kingsford Smith for a knighthood that was bestowed upon him by King George V. In October 1933 he flew back to Australia in a Percival Gull powered by a Gipsy engine in 7 days 4 hours 44 minutes to set a new solo record time.

With his own airline wound up whilst Qantas captured the sought-after route licences Kingsford Smith continued to make the headlines. In October 1934 he made the first west-to-east flight across the Pacific ocean. His co-pilot was a former Royal Flying Corps officer, Captain P.G. Taylor. The latter had originally been a sailor and held an extra master's certificate which at that time was the highest navigational qualification. They flew a Lockheed Altair monoplane powered by one Pratt and Whitney Wasp engine from Brisbane to San Francisco with stops at Fiji and Honolulu.

They had named the Altair *"Anzac"* but there were protests that this name was sacred to the memory of those who had fought at Gallipoli and should not be used for commercial purposes. The name was changed to *"Lady Southern Cross."* Kingsford Smith was very short of funds and left the Altair in California to be sold but no buyer was forthcoming. He offered *"Southern Cross"* to the Australian Government but despite the magnificent history of this machine had to be content with £1,500. It was put into storage to await the construction of an aviation museum.

Whilst he waited for the money he resorted once again to offering joyrides. Then he had *"Lady Southern Cross"* shipped to England so that he could make an attempt to lower the record time to Australia once more. He had never given up hope of obtaining a licence to resume flights to New Zealand and was a director of a company pursuing that aim. No businessman himself and with his friend Charles Ulm recently lost over the Pacific ocean, Kingsford Smith knew no other way forward but in the air.

On 6th November 1935 he flew out of Lympne with his co-pilot Tom Pethyridge. Aged 38 he was in need of a long rest from flying and was probably not in a fit state for the task that he had set himself. A few days later the lights of *"Lady Southern Cross"* were seen over Calcutta as they headed out over the Bay of Bengal. They never reached their destination. Two years later one of the wheels of their aircraft was washed up on the coast of Burma.

Kingsford Smith had not received the money for *"Southern Cross."* Five months after his death the government increased the sum to £3,000 and this was paid to his widow, Mary. That amount had been the purchase price paid in 1928. *"Southern Cross"* remained in storage for a further two years.

The verdict of Sir Hudson Fysh, chairman of Qantas, was that "Smithy was the greatest trans-world flier of them all." Others called him "a flying clown . . . a super egoist." At the time of his death the Postmaster General of New Zealand was ready to support the Trans-Tasman airmail service. But his counterpart in Australia did not share that view and called Kingsford Smith a dreamer, his plans fifteen years ahead of the times.

It was 1966 before the Australian government reminded the public of the feats of their countryman when his portrait appeared on the 20-dollar banknote.

CHAPTER 5

RAY HINCHLIFFE

FORGOTTEN AIR PIONEER

The small number of pilots who were the first to be enrolled by Imperial Airways had in earlier years flown in combat against the Germans and subsequently joined the very first British airlines in 1919. Imperial Airways was an amalgamation of four small companies struggling to compete against each other and the heavily-subsidised French and Dutch concerns. Even Germany, denied an air force under the terms of the treaty of Versailles, subsidised its airline.

When I was engaged in the research required to write the history of the infant British company I became increasingly impressed by the single-minded fortitude and dogged determination of that small band of pilots whose task it was to carry passengers and mail in a collection of converted bombers. An older generation of aviation enthusiasts can certainly recall some of their names. Sadly, one whose career ended in tragedy when he was only 33 years of age is seldom remembered. His own contribution does not deserve to be forgotten.

Walter George Raymond Hinchliffe was born in 1894, the son of a well known artist. Educated at Liverpool College he proved to be an accomplished sportsman, excelling in cricket and boxing. He won the swimming championship of Wales and was also a skilful pianist. Entering the University of Liverpool he studied for a degree in dental surgery. In 1912 he enrolled in the Territorial Army with the result that he was called up as soon as the war broke out in 1914. Two years later he transferred to the Royal Naval Air Service where his proficiency as a pilot was recognised by his employment at Cranwell as an instructor.

In 1918 Hinchliffe was posted to a squadron in France as a flight commander and was immediately engaged in day and night operations, flying Sopwith Camels over the Western Front. His log books have all been preserved by his daughter Joan and contain far more detailed information than can be found in those of most pilots. In February of that year, in the company of four other aircraft, an equal number of German Albatross scouts were encountered. In the melée Hinchliffe's left gun jammed and his engine lost power. To evade his pursuers he put his aircraft into a spin before gliding over an airfield in enemy territory. At fifty feet his engine picked up. He made for the sea at low level, dodging three enemy aircraft. He fired a burst at one of these and saw it crash into a tree.

His log book reveals details of innumerable dogfights including encounters with the triplanes of Von Richthofen's Circus. Then in 1918 he was flying alone on a night patrol to intercept intruding Gothas. When one of these was illuminated by a searchlight Hinchliffe promptly attacked it.

"During the encounter," he wrote, "I was shot in the forehead. As a result I crashed on top of a forest, fracturing my head and face."

His injuries included the permanent loss of sight of one eye but within eight weeks he was flying again.

An entry in his log reads: "Stunting. Flew upside down two circuits of aerodrome. Looped off the ground. Quite OK now. Ears well back. Tail up." He was awarded the Distinguished Flying Cross and reverted to instructional duties.

When the war ended Hinchliffe passed the medical examination for a civilian pilot's licence and was employed by A.V. Roe to fly their machines at an aviation exhibition in Amsterdam. The Dutch airline K.L.M. was in process of formation by Albert Plesman, and Hinchliffe was engaged as chief pilot. Initially K.L.M.'s fleet was made up of Avros and DH.9s. Before long Mr Fokker completed his first civilian machine, the F.2, a high-wing monoplane. Fitted with either a BMW or Mercedes engine the fuel economy was exceptional but both engines proved troublesome and Hinchliffe recorded his opinion that a Siddeley Puma would be more reliable.

Technical failures on his first four attempts to fly the F.2 to England inspired a bitter entry in his log:

"If I continue to fly with this engine there is only one result – CRASH."

In September 1920 he reached Cricklewood safely for a demonstration to the Handley Page airline. Mr Page was not impressed but his managing director, Major Woods Humphery, declared the F.2 to be "the best machine of this age."

In November an improved version, the F.3, with seating for five passengers, met with Hinchliffe's approval except for the poor forward visibility accorded to the pilot. He wrote at length to Fokker, detailing various defects which had not been remedied, and complained that Plesman had failed to pass on his recommendations. Fokker however did decide to adopt the Siddeley Puma engine and the first F.3 so fitted was delivered to K.L.M. by Gordon Olley, recruited from Handley Page. Hinchliffe's relationship with Plesman, never good, continued to deteriorate.

The personal remarks in his log book became more acid: "He is the most self-opinionated ass I have ever met."

In March 1922 Hinchliffe resigned to take up the post of chief pilot with Daimler Airway. Accompanying him to England was a Miss Emilie Gallizien, a secretary whom the pilot had frequently carried on test flights. They were married at Croydon registry office and made their home in Purley.

Daimler Airway had only been in existence for a year, the result of efforts by Major Woods Humphery to persuade the BSA-Daimler combine to put up the money after the three original airlines had all been forced to cease operations. These were Air Transport and Travel (A.T. & T.), Handley Page Transport and Instone Air Line.

At first the Chancellor of the Exchequer, Winston Churchill, had been adamant that "civil aviation must fly by itself. The government cannot possibly hold it up in the air." The result was that British taxpayers were paying for the upkeep of aerodromes, wireless and weather services used only by foreign airlines. In an early example of a government U-turn the need for subsidies had finally been conceded.

Daimler Airway obtained a few DH.18s which had been intended for the defunct A.T. & T. Following a move from Hounslow the official airport for London was Croydon. Combining two wartime R.A.F. airfields the flying area was rough, narrow and uneven with a huge dip. There were occasional incursions of sheep. When the weather at Croydon was too bad for flying the controller at Lympne fired Very lights to warn pilots inbound from the continent to land there.

When Hinchliffe flew his first service for Daimler it was in a DH.34, one of the entire fleet of three machines. This was a single-engine biplane with seating for eight passengers. It was not heated and passengers were advised to wear their overcoats. In the open cockpit the pilot and wireless operator wore helmets, goggles and heavy leather coats. The windscreen was frequently spattered with oil blown back from the engine. Blind flying instruments had not been developed. Compasses and altimeters were unreliable. At Croydon Hinchliffe was a distinctive figure for the black or pink patch he wore over one eye. It was also his practice to remove his helmet and replace it with a bowler hat when he walked from his aircraft into the terminal building.

In February 1923 he recorded "the worst trip I have ever had. Clouds almost on the ground. Halfway over the Channel the clouds reached the water. Climbed and flew between two layers. Top layer suddenly closed down and joined bottom layer. I reversed course and dived through. Came out about 200 feet above water. Now flew parallel to French coast. Eventually struck coast at Zeebrugge. Wind now 50 mph (official report). Repeatedly met clouds on surface and had to make detours. Very unpleasant indeed. Landed Schiphol in rain and wind. Only machine to fly that day."

Such experiences were by no means uncommon and one wonders what thoughts passed through the minds of the passengers. Undoubtedly the general public, very few of whom ever expected to travel by air, regarded flying as a costly and dangerous means of transport. But there were those who could afford the fares and enjoyed the opportunity to entertain their friends with exciting details of their flights.

In April 1923, flying a DH.34 to Amsterdam, Hinchliffe was approaching the Dutch coast when the engine overheated. Switching off the fuel he glided down to land on the shore of an island. With help from local people the machine was pulled away from the water. Then he and his passengers walked for an hour to obtain transport. By boat, motor car and tram they reached

Amsterdam late that night. The following day Hinchliffe returned to the aircraft, taking mechanics to dismantle it, before arranging its removal in a barge to Rotterdam.

Almost a week later he flew the inaugural service to Berlin. But most of the Company's services were to Amsterdam or Rotterdam and he was very dissatisfied with the level of technical assistance offered by his original employers, with whom the route was shared.

"One day," he wrote, "Woods Humphery will realise the futility of working with K.L.M."

He also clashed with Woods Humphery over what he regarded as pressure to operate aircraft with unremedied defects. In June of that year he made his last flight for Daimler. His log book shows that he had flown for 149 hours in thirty days over a distance of 14,000 miles.

Within a week Hinchliffe was flying for the Instone Air Line which also operated the DH.34 on the route to Brussels and Cologne. On a few occasions he flew their Vickers Vulcan. But on 31st March 1924 Instone Air Line ceased operations. The government had finally decided to merge the companies to avoid subsidising wasteful competition among themselves and thus to offer a more effective challenge to the foreign operators.

The government's "chosen instrument" was Imperial Airways. The company was allowed a monopoly on the existing route structure and was accorded a subsidy, partly dependent upon mileage flown. But the public were also invited to buy shares. Sir Eric Geddes of the Dunlop Rubber Company was appointed part-time chairman, Sir Samuel Instone one of the directors. Major Woods Humphery became general manager, Franklyn Barnard the chief pilot. The combined fleets of the three airlines required only sixteen pilots for services to begin. Hinchliffe was joined by men whose names became legendary in civil aviation, O.P. Jones, Gordon Olley, Wolley Dod, "All-weather" McIntosh and R.F. Minchin. It was not then the practice to accord the courtesy title of 'captain' to pilots so most of them chose to retain their wartime rank. Minchin had been a Lieutenant Colonel.

Services should have resumed on 1st April but the aircraft remained on the ground for several weeks. The salaries and conditions of service offered to the pilots and mechanics were markedly inferior to those previously in effect and all of them rejected the terms of the contract. A further grievance was the appointment of Woods Humphery. Invariably prepared to cope with the most daunting weather conditions many pilots recalled with resentment the pressures put upon them to fly machines with a history of repeated defects. When the conditions of service were resolved Major Brackley, formerly of Handley Page, was appointed air superintendent with direct access to the chairman as the representative of the pilots. By the time Woods Humphery had been persuaded to withdraw the writ which he had lodged against his detractors about a dozen aircraft had been made ready to begin services.

Hinchliffe recorded these events and added: "We considered that the management and general system was dangerous and we hoped that Brackley, who had been appointed to look after our interests, would carry out his duties fairly, otherwise fatal crashes would most surely take place."

It was the Company's policy that the pilots should fly all the various types so Hinchliffe was soon at the controls of the twin-engine Handley Page W.86 which seated fourteen passengers. He also flew the solitary Vickers Vimy, once the property of Instone. Sometimes he was asked to drop letters en route to his destination. These were attached to parachutes.

"One fell into a brook," he wrote, "the other in an apple tree, but both were delivered."

Particularly during winter operations flights often had to be concluded at places other than a proper airfield and Hinchliffe invariably sent picture postcards to his daughter Joan on such occasions.

One week before Christmas Day he flew a DH.34 to Amsterdam and the engine oil pressure showed a sharp fall. En route to Croydon the next day this happened again and he returned to Amsterdam. White metal was found in the filter so he suspected the bearing. There was a further recurrence on the following morning so he turned back once more. On the 23rd he encountered a tremendous storm on his way north and landed at Lympne as darkness fell. He was delayed on Christmas Eve through the aircraft having to be pulled from boggy ground. As soon as he had landed at Croydon he was instructed to fly the machine back to Paris. He refused and another pilot was ordered to take it.

"In spite in my adverse engine reports to H-, C- and S- this machine was signed out. At 12.05 the pilot took off with seven passengers. This take-off was bad and at 12.10 after vainly trying to return to the aerodrome he spun into the ground and the machine caught fire. The eight occupants were burnt to death."

Giving evidence at the enquiry Minchin said that the 1,600 yards available for take-off was insufficient and buildings on the perimeter posed an additional hazard. Barnard agreed and Brackley acknowledged that in bad weather conditions Croydon could be unsafe for flying. But Hinchliffe's verbal and written reports were rejected by the Company, which stated: "The facts did not call for more than a ground run of the engine. This was done and the fault had not been reproduced."

In March 1925 Hinchliffe flew the DH.50 for the first time. Fifteen minutes flying experience on this type was evidently considered sufficient for it to be added to his licence, after which he took off in the same machine for Amsterdam. No passengers were carried, nor were any booked on the return flight to London. The log records this with the wry comment: "Imperial only requires mileage and not passengers – for the subsidy."

The pilots became accustomed to forced landings when engine power was lost or seemed likely to fail. Hinchliffe was as experienced as others in this regard. His log book records such events, with passengers being obliged to stay overnight at a local inn. Not for the first time he had to make a forced landing between the breakwaters on a Dutch beach. Subsequently he supervised the dismantling of the machine and its transfer to Rotterdam.

This happened in the summer of 1925. His impatience with criticism from his superiors, following his delayed return to Croydon, is reflected in his written comments: "Brackley passed his usual inane remarks."

When a tyre burst when he was taxying out at Croydon, "Brackley decided that I was taxying too fast." Hinchliffe thought this uncalled for from someone who "taxies slowly but rarely flies." Months later his log continues to refer to "trouble with Brackley. This has been brewing for some time."

In October he made his first flight in the Handley Page Hampstead W.9, a three-engined machine. He conducted demonstration flights carrying, among others, Sir Sefton Brancker who was Director of Civil Aviation, and foreign air attachés. Mr Handley Page was flown the short distance from his works airfield at Cricklewood to Croydon: "Extremely nervous, no doubt due to his having seen the machine being built." Sir Eric Geddes made his first-ever flight in this new machine with Hinchliffe, accompanied by Woods Humphery and Brackley. "Everyone appeared to be satisfied." Imperial Airways accepted delivery of the W.9 but bought only one further one. In the following year four W.10 machines, each with two Napier engines, proved to be more reliable.

In the summer of 1926 Armstrong Whitworth began delivery of their three-engined Argosy aircraft to the Company. These could carry twenty passengers but their cruising speed of 95 mph was little faster than their other machines. In December the first of the de Havilland DH.66 Hercules entered service. In customary fashion Hinchliffe was flying passenger services within a couple of days of his introduction to the type. The Hercules was intended to operate the new route between Cairo and India. Hinchliffe and Wolley Dod flew the first two machines to Egypt. Ten landings were made en route in a flying time of 26 hours. The two pilots returned by sea.

Such journeys, all too rare, made a welcome change from regular services to the same four European cities. Boredom with such work was setting in. Carrying six passengers to Zurich Hinchliffe observed an army officer galloping a horse around the aerodrome. He made a low pass over the rider who fell off his mount. There were official complaints which earned the pilot suspension from further flights to Zurich.

The summer of 1927 witnessed the arrival in Paris from New York of Charles Lindbergh in a Ryan monoplane *"Spirit of St. Louis."* This was the first non-stop flight by a solitary pilot across the Atlantic from North America. Two weeks later an even longer flight was accomplished by Clarence Chamberlin in a Bellanca. He landed just short of Berlin as his fuel was running out. He was accompanied by his sponsor, Charles Levine.

These achievements encouraged a number of airmen to attempt the first east-to-west crossing of the Atlantic and thereby to win the substantial sums on offer to the successful pilot. Both Minchin and Hinchliffe were interested but it was the former who made the first attempt. He had a fine record of service to Imperial Airways and had undertaken the proving flights to India, flying into every possible landing ground which might be useful on the proposed airline route. But in June, en route to Croydon from Paris, his machine ran out of fuel and suffered damage in a forced landing. It was repaired and remained in service for several more years but Minchin was blamed and dismissed. The Board of the Company were made aware that Minchin intended to try and fly across the Atlantic. The minutes of a meeting reveal that his dismissal was to be reconsidered after his attempt.

Sadly Minchin, his navigator and their sponsor lost their lives as so many others had done. But Hinchliffe had a particular motive in facing the same challenge at that time. He had good reason to fear that tougher medical standards shortly to be introduced for commercial pilots would inevitably exclude anyone who had lost their sight from an eye. His first plan was to accompany Charles Chamberlin to North America in the Bellanca but this fell through. Charles Levine however agreed to allow Hinchliffe to fly the machine and to make a record-breaking flight to India.

They set out together on 23rd September. On 4th October they took off from Rome where Prince Bourbon had been taken on board. Soon after take-off the engine cut out completely and on landing a wheel collapsed. Levine lost all further interest in their endeavour so Hinchliffe returned to routine flying with Imperial Airways.

But the date of his next medical examination was fast approaching. He faced unemployment with no means of supporting his family. There was an urgent need for him to find a sponsor for the Atlantic flight and he found one in the person of the Hon. Elsie Mackay, daughter of the Earl of Inchcape, who was herself a private pilot. She provided the money for Hinchliffe to sail to the United States and to choose a suitable aircraft. Whilst he was in New York his wife gave birth to a second daughter.

The machine which Hinchliffe chose was a Stinson monoplane but various deceptions had to be employed. The manufacturers were later to claim that they had demanded an undertaking that the Stinson was not intended for an Atlantic crossing. The fuel capacity was insufficient for such a venture. Elsie Mackay's chief concern was that her father should not be made aware of her plans. An R.A.F. officer was prevailed upon to pretend that he was to act as navigator and sole companion on Hinchliffe's flight. The Stinson was shipped to Southampton and on 18th February 1928 he tested it at Weybridge. Six days later Hinchliffe flew to Cranwell, chosen because it possessed the longest runway, essential to an aircraft loaded to its limit with fuel.

On the 29th Hinchliffe entered in his log. "My confidence in the success of our venture now 100%." It was the last entry he was to make.

Elsie Mackay wanted none of the prize money for herself. Her greatest wish was to share the acclaim which would be accorded to the successful aviators. She had promised to insure Hinchliffe's life for £10,000 and to pay the substantial premium to the insurers prior to their departure. The need to take off as soon as possible became urgent. Cranwell was an R.A.F. station and the station commander became uneasy at the interest and intrusions of the Press. The Stinson had already been damaged by someone seeking a memento. The weather situation in February was a worrying factor. Elsie Mackay was increasingly alarmed that her father would become aware of her intentions.

They took off on 13th March. Hinchliffe's pilot's licence was invalid; his medical clearance should have been obtained two weeks earlier. He omitted to take with him his log book or his passport. The monoplane was capable of a speed of 130 mph but the prevailing westerly wind over the North Atlantic would have reduced that very considerably. Probably thirty hours would pass before the coast of Newfoundland could be reached. An amateur wireless operator claimed to have heard a message from a French ship which reported sighting the aircraft off Ireland. The hours passed by with no news of its progress. Many months later a tyre and a portion of an undercarriage were washed up on the west coast of Ireland. These were positively identified as having come from the Stinson.

Newspaper reports at the time said that:

"Captain Walter Hinchliffe, and Hon. Elsie Mackay, daughter of Lord Inchcape, his companion on the sensational Atlantic flight from Cranwell (Lincolnshire) have not been reported late on Wednesday afternoon.

At 4 pm the fliers were 37 hours out from Cranwell in their Stinson monoplane *"Endeavour,"* and eight hours overdue. They should have crossed the Newfoundland coast at 8 am.

New York is approximately 1,150 miles from St. Johns (Newfoundland) or, in flying time, 11½ hours away."

" . . . elaborate measures were taken to hoodwink outsiders.

Captain Hinchliffe, the Hon. Elsie Mackay and Mr Gordon Sinclair stayed at the same hotel at Grantham. The night porter called them at 4 am. All were dressed in full flying kit. The porter says he noticed flying breeches beneath Miss Mackay's fur coat.

The three drove to the aerodrome in Miss Mackay's motor, taking three days' provisions, which were loaded on the aeroplane."

" . . . when the party entered a motor car to drive to the aerodrome, Miss Mackay was pale and overcome. She waved her hand in farewell, but seemed unable to speak.

Thirty-four, dark and pretty, steel-nerved, whether she is astride a horse, piloting an aeroplane, or being "shot" for the movies, describes Hon. Elsie Mackay, who is better known to the screen as Poppy Wyndham.

Now as the companion of Captain Hinchliffe on his Atlantic flight she is rivetting the attention of the biggest audience of her sensational career."

Meanwhile the tragedy for Hinchliffe's family was intensified by their failure to receive any financial compensation from the insurers. The Earl of Inchcape was trustee for his daughter's estate and acted so swiftly that even the premium due to the insurance company was frozen before payment. As for Imperial Airways Hinchliffe's venture formed no part of his airline duties. The Royal

Air Force also denied liability since he was not a serving officer nor a member of the R.A.F. Reserve.

Sir Sefton Brancker took up the case for Mrs Hinchliffe, persuading both Lord Beaverbrook and the proprietor of the Northcliffe Press, through their newspapers, to publicize the plight of her family. Lord Inchcape did not at first respond but as the pressure upon him increased he set up a Mackay Fund which would gather interest for fifty years and then be offered as a donation to the British government to reduce the national debt. Winston Churchill was the Chancellor of the Exchequer and while welcoming the generosity of the gift told Mrs Hinchliffe's sympathisers in the House of Commons that he had no authority to direct any grant to her. Finally Lord Inchcape placed £10,000 at the disposal of Winston Churchill to be devoted to "sufferers from the disaster," a clear reference to Mrs Hinchliffe and her children.

In the 1950s when her father's log books came into the possession of Joan Hinchliffe her wish to write a biography was frustrated by the lack of detail and loss of interest through the passage of time. Opinions on the wisdom of undertaking the final flight were offered with the advantage of hindsight.

Sir Geoffrey de Havilland said: "Looking back one realises that it was full of danger considering the weather and time of the year."

The general opinion among members of the Guild of Air Pilots was that the machine had encountered severe icing difficulties beyond anything known at that time.

Major Woods Humphery was characteristically blunt. "I could never understand why, with their brains and with futures in front of them like Hinchliffe and Barnard had, they wanted to go in for these stunts that were accompanied by such colossal risks – such a waste."

The answer to that seems to be that Hinchliffe did not see a future for himself as a commercial pilot once he had appeared before his next medical board.

But let his daughter Joan have the last word. For her father, "the prospect of continuing indefinitely to be a sort of aerial taxi driver was somewhat unattractive."

CHAPTER 6

GORDON OLLEY'S AIR SERVICE

Before flying a modern airliner comes to be regarded as a commonplace, even tedious, occupation it would be well to recall the skill and perseverance of those who played a part in the birth of British civil aviation from its earliest days and even beyond the second World War.

Gordon Olley answered the call to arms in August 1914. Attracted to aviation he flew as a corporal observer. Armed with a pistol it was one of his duties to take pot-shots at any German machine within his range. Accepted for pilot training he went solo after three hours instruction. He was commissioned and credited with shooting down 13 enemy aircraft, for which he was awarded the Military Medal.

On demobilisation he obtained work with Handley Page. With all wartime contracts cancelled Sir Frederick and a skeleton staff were converting their 0/400 bomber to carry passengers to the continent. The first commercial flight of Handley Page Transport took off from the works field at Cricklewood for Brussels in July 1919. The HP. 0/400 was a biplane powered by two Rolls Royce Eagle engines. The company's publicity stressed the extra safety provided by two engines but when one failed the pilot was obliged to make a forced landing as the aircraft could no longer maintain altitude.

Many flights were eventful. En route to Paris Olley was faced with a fuel feed problem and landed seventeen times in fields to restore the flow. On another occasion he landed near a Belgian monastery. He and his passengers were hospitably accommodated in the monks' cells. It was a time when passengers had to possess an adventurous spirit because forced landings were not uncommon. Sitting in an open cockpit, his windscreen streaked with oil from the engine, the pilot depended upon his sight of the ground for navigation. Often he had to fly at very low altitudes following railway lines, looking for familiar landmarks and avoiding church spires.

In 1921 Handley Page Transport and two other British companies attempting, unsubsidised, to compete with State-supported European airlines, were forced to abandon scheduled services until the government could be persuaded to offer help. Olley was engaged to demonstrate a DH.9 at Schipol where he met the one-eyed ex-Royal Flying Corps pilot Ray Hinchliffe, then employed by K.L.M. Olley was also enrolled and flew K.L.M.'s first service between Croydon and Amsterdam. This was in a Fokker, equipped with an Armstrong Siddeley Puma engine. It was a high-wing monoplane, of wooden construction, described as "luxuriously equipped."

When Imperial Airways was formed in 1924 following the amalgamation of the British companies Olley was one of the small group of 16 pilots who were engaged. During the inter-war years their names were to become widely known to the British public. They included Captains Horsey, O.P. Jones, R. Hinchliffe, "All-weather" McIntosh and Wilcockson. The constitution of Imperial Airways stipulated that the aircraft should be of British construction. The pilots were expected to fly each of the various types acquired. Thus Olley would have gained experience on the Handley Page W.8 and W.10, the DH.34 and DH.66, the Armstrong Whitworth Argosy and Atalanta.

Imperial Airways undertook charters when an aircraft was available and in 1927 Olley was placed in charge of their world-wide charter operations. He himself built up a good reputation among satisfied customers. These included the ruler of a sheikh-dom in the Persian gulf, big-game hunters bound for Kenya and King Albert of Belgium for a return flight to Khartoum. Another customer was the American millionaire Jock Whitney. The latter initially engaged Olley to convey his party to Paris but was so impressed by the pilot's all round ability and agreeable personality that he retained his services for a 30-day jaunt round Europe that included Berlin, Munich and Vienna.

Another millionaire, Albert Löwenstein, engaged Olley to recommend and supervise improvements to an aerodrome near Biarritz where the financier owned 40 villas and kept a number of his own private aeroplanes. He too found Olley to be a most delightful companion and demanded his presence at his billiard table or for a game of bridge late into the night. A summons long before dawn was a routine experience. The jockey Gordon Richards urgently required air transport for himself and two other riders to Ayr racecourse the following morning. Olley obliged but found the racecourse and the surrounding area totally obscured by low cloud. He flew west and descended when he was certain that he was flying over the ocean before reversing course to find the Scottish coast.

A West End theatre had engaged the French entertainer Josephine Baker but she had failed to appear as the day of her appearance dawned. Olley flew to Paris to collect her and found that she had injured her leg and could not dance.

"But you are known to be a wonderful singer," he told her. "You will have the sympathy of your audience who will greatly appreciate your appearance on stage to sing to them."

Thus convinced she flew to Croydon with Olley, who was among a delighted audience that night.

Edward, Prince of Wales, was a passenger on numerous occasions, liking to sit alongside the pilot. Olley once brought him home from Paris, flying the three-engined Armstrong Whitworth Argosy for a landing on the polo ground on Smith's Lawn, Windsor.

A publicity stunt organised by Imperial Airways did not turn out so well. The object was to encourage passengers to Scotland to travel by air. A flight to Edinburgh was scheduled to depart from Croydon at the same time that the *"Flying Scotsman"* steamed out of Euston station. Olley was accompanied by an engine-driver whilst another pilot was on the footplate of the locomotive. The *"Flying Scotsman"* operated a non-stop service to Scotland but Olley had to land twice to refuel. It was intended that he should fly directly above the train as it crossed the Royal Border Bridge over the river Tweed at Berwick. Photographers were in position to take pictures of the event.

Unfortunately he was tracking the wrong train, which passed over the bridge five minutes after the *"Flying Scotsman"* had already done so. His engine-driver companion realised the error when this train stopped at a station. Olley increased speed, fearful of arriving late at his destination. After landing his passengers were hastily despatched to greet those disembarking from the train. The latter were already waiting on the platform.

In April 1933 Imperial Airways came to an agreement with the Great Western Railway to supply aircraft, pilots and engineers to run a domestic service within the British Isles. This was a wise move since the main railway companies had obtained parliamentary authority to operate services both within the United Kingdom and to the continent. The first aircraft allotted was a Westland Wessex, G-AAGW, which seated six passengers. Olley flew the inaugural services from Cardiff to Plymouth. This arrangement with the G.W.R. was subsequently extended to include the London, Midland and Scottish Railway, the London and North Eastern Railway and the Southern Railway. The final outcome was the formation of Railway Air Services under the patronage of Imperial Airways. Operations began in 1934; the aircraft employed were the DH.84 Dragon, the DH.86 Express and the DH.89 Dragon Rapide. R.A.S. operated only within the United Kingdom and did not compete with Imperial Airways to the continent.

With these arrangements in place Gordon Olley resigned from Imperial Airways to found his own airline, Olley Air Service. This venture was backed by Sir Hugo Cunliffe Owen and Sir James Dunn. His headquarters were in Lower Belgrave Street, close to Victoria Station. With DH Dragons and Rapides Olley operated charter flights and scheduled services to Deauville, Le Touquet and Luxembourg, from Croydon and Shoreham. The outbreak of war in 1939 brought upheaval to all airlines. Those that continued to operate inside the United Kingdom were represented by the Associated Airways Joint Committee. Olley was made operations manager, based at Speke Airport.

After the war, when he was permitted to operate an independent airline again, he resumed services with two Dragon Rapides and acquired two more, in addition to two Airspeed Consuls, for the summer season. In 1947 a French railway strike enabled Olley to gain revenue bringing back stranded holiday-makers from the continent. He then bought two DH Doves, which were often seen at racecourses in Britain and abroad.

Ronald Gillman, a fighter pilot demobilised after the war, wrote about his application for a job with Olley. He had arrived at Croydon from Scotland at 7 pm the Thursday before Easter Day. He enquired at a ticket desk where Olley could be found and discovered the latter to be still in his office. After scrutinising Gillman's log book Olley enquired when he would be free to start work.

"Easter Monday?" Gillman suggested tentatively.

"Be here by nine," he was told.

On that day he was ushered on to the DH.86 Express, the first four-engined aircraft that he had ever encountered. He performed six landings to the satisfaction of his employer and was then given a thorough introduction to the control, fuel and oil systems and other parts of the aircraft by an engineer. Next he was introduced to the Air Registration Board official based at Croydon who submitted Gillman to an oral test of his knowledge of the aircraft. At this juncture Olley reappeared.

"All done?" he asked. "Then the appropriate documents will be put in this post to the Ministry and it will be legal. You can take out the afternoon flight to Liverpool."

At that time a competent pilot in possession of a civil 'B' licence could obtain employment without great difficulty. In the months that followed very many more pilots released from the R.A.F. passed the examination and competed for what jobs remained. Gillman flew the DH.86 with one other crew member, a wireless operator. The aircraft was not equipped with a standard beam approach (SBA) receiver. Just as Olley had done when trying to find Ayr racecourse many years earlier, Gillman taught himself what heading to fly over some prominent landmark and how many seconds to fly on that heading before turning on to another and beginning his descent. Over the ocean it was the practice for the wireless operator to wind out the trailing aerial and report when he heard on his earphones the crackle as the end of it struck the sea.

In 1953 Morton Air Services acquired all the share capital of Olley's airline but the latter remained as Managing Director until his death on 18th March 1958. He had accumulated 13,500 flying hours in a career lasting 44 years.

"The Times" published an obituary as follows:

"Captain Gordon Percy Olley, M.M., an outstanding pilot of aircraft, died yesterday in hospital at Wimbledon. He began flying in 1915 and by 1931 had flown 1,000,000 miles – over 12,000 hours – and had carried safely 14,000 passengers. He was a familiar figure during the years he flew for Imperial Airways; later he gave his name to Olley Air Service Ltd., of which firm he became managing director. He had on many occasions flown members of the Royal Family.

Olley enlisted in the R.F.C. in 1914, was for a time an air mechanic, and went to France before being accepted for training as a pilot and receiving a commission. After active service on the Western Front he came home to England and carried out acceptance trrials of new aircraft. In 1919 he joined Handley Page Transport on the first Continental air services, and in 1921 started the first servce between England and Holland with K.L.M. Three years later he took up employment with Imperial Airways, and "G.P.O.," with his small, compact figure, quick movements and trim moustache, was known to thousands of regular air travellers. Subsequently he was placed in charge of the special charter department of Imperial Airways, flying anything from bullion to big-game hunters to all parts of the world. He was a versatile flyer, who set up a duration record in a Fokker glider in 1922."

CHAPTER 7

ALAN COBHAM

A LIFETIME OF SERVICE TO AVIATION

Alan Cobham's career as a pioneer airman and subsequent inventor of in-flight refuelling came about as a consequence of the first World War. His main interest had been in farm animals and when he volunteered his services in 1914 he was welcomed into the Army Veterinary Corps and swiftly promoted to sergeant. Three years on the Western Front made him aware of the increasing use and importance of aircraft. Here was the growth industry of the future and he was attracted. He transferred to the Royal Flying Corps as a cadet pilot.

Cobham's resolve to remain in aviation after the surrender of Germany was not blunted by the knowledge that the aircraft manufacturers were laying off their own test pilots and that there were thousands of demobilised pilots. In partnership with two brothers enough money was borrowed to buy an Avro 504K from the government's disposal company and to offer joyrides to the public. For a time the business flourished. Another pilot, one O.P. Jones, was engaged. Then three weeks of continuous rain in the spring of 1920 decimated their financial resources. Cobham pulled out while he could still pay his debts.

He was not unemployed for long. Holt Thomas, founder of the Aircraft Manufacturing Company (AIRCO) had anticipated a future in aerial photography after the end of hostilities and Cobham was engaged to fly a DH.9 in the company of a photographer. This activity was profitable but when AIRCO was put into liquidation the photography department was sold to a company called Aerofilms. The latter owned no aircraft but chartered them. When de Havilland offered their services Aerofilms had heard enough about Cobham's ability to insist that he was employed.

Working for de Havilland in 1921 were several other young men as youthful as himself, each of whom achieved fame in their own fields. R.E. Bishop became the company's Chief Designer, H. Hardingham the Chief Executive of the Air Registration Board. H. Tiltman was to design the Airspeed Envoy and Courier. Nevil Shute Norway helped to design the airship R.100 and was subsequently a best-selling author. In addition to aerial photography air-taxi journeys were flown, frequently on behalf of newspapers. In addition Cobham delivered aircraft ordered by customers in Spain. Geoffrey de Havilland recognised the talent of his new recruit and in March 1922 the latter flew the DH.34 airliner on its first test flight.

The following year he flew the DH.50 to Gothenburg for an aeronautical exhibition where it won the first prize in the reliability trials. Severe competition came from an all-metal low-wing monoplane entered by Junkers. Cobham observed that technically it was in advance of anything being built in Britiain. He was also very impressed by its German pilot. His name was Hermann Goering.

The Director of Civil Aviation, Sir Sefton Brancker, was due to go to India in 1924 to arrange for the installation of mooring masts and hangars for the proposed airship service planned for future Empire routes. When Cobham heard that Brancker would be required to travel by sea he thought this inappropriate and urged the Air Minister to arrange for the Director to fly out on a de Havilland aircraft. This was ruled out on the grounds of cost. With typical persistence Cobham persuaded his contacts in the aviation business to make up the excess over the fare by sea. Brancker was delighted and appointed Cobham as his pilot for the flight.

The aircraft used was a DH.50 G-EBFO, which could carry four passengers in an enclosed cabin. The pilot sat in a cockpit open to the weather. He took with him a mechanic, Elliott. They flew out of Stag Lane on 20th November and ten days and twelve landings later arrived in Karachi. This achievement is best appreciated when it is realised that blind flying instruments did not then exist. The pilot was provided with a compass, altimeter and an airspeed indicator; there was no artificial horizon. Cobham would not have been supplied with up-to-date weather reports or forecasts nor did the aircraft carry a wireless receiver. Brancker decided to extend the flight to Delhi and Rangoon. They arrived back in England in March 1925.

Imperial Airways, founded in 1924, was de Havilland's principal customer. Although passenger services to Europe were very limited the aircraft manufacturer decided to wind down his competing air-taxi business. Cobham believed that the greatest potential for an airline service lay in Africa. The entire route from Alexandria to Cape Town was in territory under British control. He asked Geoffrey de Havilland to lend him G-EBFO for a flight to the Cape and back and received his consent.

In order to cope with the extra power required for a take-off at places situated at high levels Cobham was offered the 385 horse power Jaguar engine manufactured by Sir John Siddeley. He was also successful in soliciting support from others in the aviation industry. Sir Charles Wakefield agreed to make Castrol oil supplies available along Cobham's planned route. B.P. provided petrol. Disused wartime airfields lay along the Nile. Further south playing fields and racecourses would have to serve. Spare parts had to be shipped by boat, train and on the heads of native porters. Months of meticulous preparation was carried out. It was decided to have a film of the journey made; Gaumont-British, whose newsreels were shown on the screens of almost every British cinema, provided a cameraman, B. Emmott, with the necessary equipment.

Cobham, Elliott and Emmott set off on 15th November 1925. On reaching Athens the pistons of the engine were found to be disintegrating. A week passed before 14 new pistons arrived by rail and steamer. Severe turbulence had been encountered on the Mediterranean coast from the northern winds running down from the Alps and again over the Gulf of Corinth. Without restraining straps Elliott and Emmott had been flung about the cabin. Only when they were flying south from Cairo did the possibility of a future scheduled service seem a commercial possibility.

Paddle steamers moved along the Nile at only four knots. Where roads existed they were poor. It was the dry season over much of the route. Thereafter, during the rains, grass or earth airfields would become bogs. Cobham reached Cape Town in 27 stages; he was met by a huge crowd, excited by the prospect that during their lifetime the journey between Britain and their homeland could be completed in a matter of weeks.

On 13th March 1926, when he arrived back in England, Cobham recognised that before a scheduled commercial service could become a reality airliners would have to be powered by three reliable engines. One of the pilots would have to be a qualified navigator. A good weather-reporting service would need to be established, also a system of rapid refuelling – the dependence on masses of small cans of petrol would not suffice. Meanwhile his next venture was at the forefront of his mind. He would fly to Australia in the same DH.50 but with the aircraft converted into a seaplane.

Cobham was aware that on both the outward and return journeys he would be flying over India and Burma during the monsoon season. From Calcutta to Darwin there were very few adequate airfields. Once again Geoffrey de Havilland offered his active support as did Sir Charles Wakefield. B.P., the Burma Oil Company and Shell-Mex all agreed to lay down stocks of petrol when required, from the patriotic motive of supporting a pioneer British project. The advance planning, in addition to the procurement and distribution of spares, involved poring over maps to choose suitable rivers, estuaries, harbours and lakes as places to alight. As Cobham had never flown a seaplane he went to Short's works at Rochester to obtain some practice.

So on 30th June 1926 he and Elliott were on their way once more. Emmott had to be left behind because the substitution of metal floats in place of the wheels had made the aircraft very much heavier. The fuel capacity had also been increased.

Cobham knew that many difficulties would be encountered. He could not have foreseen the tragedy that befell the pair after they left Baghdad for Basra. Dust storms forced them down to about 50 feet to make map-reading possible. Suddenly there was an explosion and Elliott reported that he was bleeding profusely. Basra had to be reached before Elliott could receive attention and on arrival Cobham beached the aircraft in a mudbank. Hours passed before Elliott could be taken to hospital where it was found that he had been hit by a bullet. He died that night and Cobham's first reaction was to abandon his journey.

Then he received cables from his wife, the Air Minister, Brancker, Wakefield and Siddeley, all urging him to carry on. The R.A.F. offered a mechanic, Sergeant Ward, as a substitute for Elliott. Cobham overcame his distress and agreed to continue the flight. When he put down at Port Darwin he had completed 23 stages since leaving England. To read his own account of the journey it is clear that in addition to the expected worries over weather and unserviceability his problems did not end when the opportunity for rest occurred. Invariably the local governor or colonial officer demanded his presence at an elaborate ceremony and the tired pilot had to put on his dinner jacket and respond to speeches of welcome. At Darwin he was met by the Director of Civil Aviation for Australia who had travelled almost 2,000 miles by train from Melbourne.

Rather than fly around the coastline of Australia Cobham had arranged to replace the floats with the original wheels. He had expected to follow the telegraph lines along his planned route but soon discovered that their thin metal posts were invisible from the air and that only the clearing in the bush through which the telegraph lines ran provided any sort of aid to navigation. There were no adequate maps of the interior of the continent.

When they landed at Newcastle Waters, one of the loneliest parts of Australia, they were met by the postmaster, a policeman and a few other men. No women lived there. Assistance was readily given in carrying cans of petrol but no conversation ensued. Cobham asked if he and Ward could remain overnight. The postmaster nodded in agreement. The response to a further request for a lift was met by a gesture in the direction of an old car. Soon afterwards they dined off tin plates with their hosts in total silence. After their previous experience of formal reception committees Cobham found the prolonged silences very restful.

The flight was continued south over featureless landscape. Navigation proved extremely difficult but the land itself served as a huge natural aerodrome, flat and dry. Help was willingly offered at cattle stations before they reached the mining district and mountainous area near Cloncurry. On then to Longreach and Charleville, the last 100 miles over a vast forest. That day they had flown 825 miles. There remained 700 miles to be flown to Sydney with stops at Bourke and Narrowmine.

At Sydney a huge crowd awaited them, the mayor unable to read his address of welcome until a free fight among press photographers had been quelled. Cobham was once more in the throes of hectic social events with speeches on each of the four days before their journey concluded in Melbourne. Here a crowd of 150,000 had assembled to witness the arrival of the DH.50. Undoubtedly Cobham provided an immense stimulus to Australian aviation. The de Havilland Cirrus Moth was already being built under licence:with his arrival new aeroplane clubs were formed at Melbourne, Sydney and Adelaide.

Their return to Darwin was via Adelaide, Oonadatta and Alice Springs. At Darwin the floats were refitted to the aircraft. Thereafter the monsoon rains over Burma and India made navigation even more difficult than during the journey eastward. When they reached Paris a telegram from the Air Minister, Sir Samuel Hoare, asked Cobham to land on the Thames at Westminster in front of the Houses of Parliament at 2 pm. En route he flew over the seaplane works at Rochester where three months earlier the metal floats had been fitted to his machine. As he circled overhead he could see the upraised faces of every employee.

Conducted up the landing stairs to the terrace of the House of Commons, Cobham was met by Hoare, Brancker, Wakefield, de Havilland and the Speaker in addition to his wife. The date was 1st October, 1926. He told the story of this journey in his book *"Australia and Back."* He failed to mention that his achievement was rewarded by a knighthood.

The limitations of seaplanes was one lesson that Cobham had learned. The sea can be dangerous, both in conditions too calm and too rough. A glossy surface makes judgement of height over the water very difficult. Where there are waves a crosswind take-off or landing has to be made across the line of the approaching waves, not along it. This presents the added danger of losing lateral control and dipping a wing. The waters of the Persian Gulf from Basra through to Karachi proved unsuitable for seaplanes.

Whereas, after touchdown, the engines of a landplane can be switched off and chocks placed in position, the seaplane has to be manoeuvred onto a buoy. For lack of a buoy assistance was required from untutored men in launches or standing waist-deep in water. The possibility of damage through collision with other craft was ever present. Cobham concluded that seaplanes or flying boats would have to be very much larger than a DH.50. They would require proper bases with the right equipment and trained staff.

He had become a celebrity but as far as de Havilland was concerned he remained a pilot in their employ; he was not invited to join the board of directors. At the suggestion of Sir John Siddeley he formed Alan Cobham Aviation Ltd. Sir Sefton Brancker told him that Imperial Airways served Cairo on their route east to India but would not be further extending their services to the rest of Africa. Air routes there and elsewhere were available to private enterprise. In fact, an old friend, Tony Blackburn, had already begun to plan such a service; he and Cobham then joined forces to bring into existence Cobham-Blackburn Air Lines Ltd.

Short Brothers had completed the trials of a Singapore flying boat for the government. Sir Samuel Hoare agreed to lend it to Cobham and once again other forward-looking figures in the aviation industry offered their backing. A New Zealander, Capt. Worrall, was engaged as second pilot; Lady Cobham found a mechanic and cameraman to act as secretary and general factotum. The Singapore was the first flying boat in the world to be constructed entirely of metal. Cobham and Worrall liked it but found it very heavy on the controls. In the late winter of 1927 they set off to combine a proving flight with negotiations with the colonial governments.

The venture almost came to an end in Malta. Poor handling by a towboat wrenched off a float. Gales and high seas caused further damage, necessitating spares from England. It was the 21st January before Cobham was off again via Benghazi for Alexandria. Talks with the authorities in Egypt, Sudan, Kenya, Rhodesia and Tanganyika all went well. From Cape Town the route home was along the Atlantic coast. But after leaving Abidjan for Sierra Leone the port engine vibrated so violently that Cobham alighted on a lagoon.

An inspection found the crankcase to be practically broken in two. With great difficulty a cable was sent to Rolls Royce requesting a new engine. On 15th May it was possible to resume the flight to Freetown. Three months later than the planned date Cobham touched down at Plymouth. On the final short hop to Rochester the crankcase of the starboard Condor engine broke, necessitating an emergency landing at Calshot.

Undeterred by these setbacks and encouraged by Sir Samuel Hoare, Cobham tried to generate enthusiasm for airline services to the Empire. He held discussions with cabinet ministers and the chairmen of established shipping companies. Their response was uniformly depressing. Lord Birkenhead, Secretary of State for India, took comfort from the knowledge that a despatch to the subcontinent could not generate a reply in less than seven weeks. The thought that an aeroplane could bring it back in a matter of days appalled him. Nor were the chairmen of Union Castle and the P. & O. cooperative. Cobham had suggested that their overseas staff could act as agencies for ticketing. Little did they realise that civil aviation would deprive them of their passengers so soon.

Meanwhile Imperial Airways put pressure on the government, insisting that their new route to India should be complemented by the exclusive right to services within Africa. Despite Cobham's protestations that he and Blackburn had made the proving flight Imperial Airways won the day and Cobham-Blackburn was wound up in July 1930.

Cobham's enthusiasm for promoting civil aviation was never destroyed by such setbacks. His next project was to persuade every major British city and town to choose a suitable site for a municipal airport before residential or industrial development spread too far from the centre. In a tour lasting five months he flew a DH.61 single-engined biplane to 110 locations, taking civil dignitaries on flights to view their homes from above. Sir Charles Wakefield paid for about 10,000 schoolchildren to be carried on short flights.

The tour was only a partial success. Cobham received many commissions to inspect sites. Hurn and Speke eventually became important centres of aviation but at a time when the R.A.F. was pitifully underfunded there was little parliamentary support for public expenditure on municipal airports.

So another project came into being. From his base at Ford aerodrome on the coast of Sussex Cobham assembled a fleet of aircraft both for joyriding and to carry out aerobatic and other displays. His circus toured the British Isles. One of these machines was an Airspeed Ferry, a three-engined biplane specifically designed for Cobham by Nevil Shute Norway. The Ferry provided easy access and exit for passengers with good downward visibility from the windows. These were built in a former bus garage and certificated in record time. Other aircraft ranged from the Handley Page W.10, described as "a giant airliner," an Avro 504K, Desoutter, Comper Swift, Southern Martlet, Handley Page Clive, D.H. Moth and an Autogiro.

The first display took place on 12th April 1932 and continued through successive summers until 1935. The date of the event was billed at each location as "National Aviation Day." About four million people attended the displays of whom almost a quarter paid for a flight. Several years later, when the R.A.F. were recruiting pilots from thousands of young volunteers it was apparent that many had made their one and only flight at one of these displays.

These events took place before the onset of winter when the circus moved to South Africa. A DH.66 was borrowed from Imperial Airways who benefited from the publicity. Sir John Siddeley lent Armstrong Whitworth aircraft and Armstrong Siddeley cars to boost local sales. The South African tours were not profitable but achieved Cobham's purpose of bringing aviation to the people and making them air-minded. In 1935 he sold the display to C.W.A. Scott (who had won the Mildenhall - Melbourne air race) without the right to use his name.

For at least a decade Cobham had reflected upon the fact that an aircraft required far more power to take off from the ground than to sustain it in the air. The take-off and climb consumed a large amount of fuel, thus reducing its range. This could be greatly extended if the aircraft was flown off with a full payload but little fuel, and could then have its tanks replenished in flight.

In 1931, in the early days of Airspeed, Cobham and his fellow director N.S. Norway had experimented with a hose dangling behind a tanker aircraft. They found that it lashed about so that a method of weighting had to be devised. The solution proved to be a bag full of water that would not damage a propeller. Norway then designed the Airspeed Courier, a single-engine low-wing aeroplane. Using an old bomber as a tanker Cobham flew the Courier alongside the dangling bag. Bill Helmore, later to become an Air Commodore, grabbed the hose and plugged it into the Courier's tank. Using gravity alone 120 gallons of fuel were transferred in only one minute.

After a great number of trials Cobham founded Flight Refuelling Ltd on 1st January 1936. By then he had reached an agreement with Imperial Airways to refuel their Short Empire flying boats in a series of flights across the North Atlantic. Refuelling stations were established at Shannon in Ireland and Gander, Newfoundland. At each of these an old Harrow bomber was positioned to act as a tanker. Imperial Airways modified "Cabot" and "Caribou" to receive fuel in the air.

After take-off from the Foynes river the flying boat climbed to the selected cruising level, usually no more than 2,000 feet, and was refuelled. It then flew westward into the prevailing wind non-stop to Botwood in Newfoundland. A token payload of newspapers and films was sometimes carried but no passengers. On the eastbound flight home the flying boat was refuelled from Gander. Sixteen crossings were made before the second World War put an end to the trials.

A further blow to Cobham's business was the requisitioning by the Admiralty of Ford aerodrome in 1940. He was able to find alternative sites for the work assigned to him at Staverton aerodrome and in the Malvern hills. Aware that the Short Sunderlands of Coastal Command did not have the range to protect convoys from U-boats over much of the Atlantic ocean Cobham tried to convince the Air Ministry that the principle of flight refuelling should be adopted. He was rebuffed and finally gave up when he heard two Air Marshals observe his approach and heard one remark to the other: "Oh God! Here comes Cobham with his bloody refuelling . . . I'll leave it to you to get rid of him."

In 1946 a new airline, British South American Airways, began to operate the longest non-stop ocean crossing in the world, from the Azores to Bermuda. Avro Lancastrians were being used prior to the introduction of A.V. Roe's Tudor. The Airline's chief, Air Vice Marshal Bennett, had participated in the prewar North Atlantic trials as an Imperial Airways captain. He welcomed the cooperation with Cobham on this new venture and personally commanded the first non-stop flight to Bermuda with Cobham on board. The tanker aircraft was another Lancaster, based in the Azores. This was the first of 22 such flights.

Despite their success no airline ever adopted flight refuelling. The range of commercial airliners had been extended by the introduction of Lockheed Constellations, Boeing Stratocruisers and Douglas DC-6s. Cobham might have gone out of business if a United States committee, chaired by General Doolittle, had not been determined to ensure that the Americans should possess bombers with an intercontinental range. The General was unwilling to wait several years for such bombers to be produced. He knew that Cobham was the man to overcome this problem and the latter was able to satisfy him.

When a further request came for a means of refuelling fighters Cobham's team again came up with a solution. This was a hose with a funnel-shaped drogue on the end. The fighter was fitted with a long probe on its nose. By 1949 a Gloster Meteor was kept aloft for 12 hours and the following year the U.S.A.F. flew an F-84 non-stop across the Atlantic ocean.

Today Sir Michael Cobham continues the work of his multi-talented father. Flight Refuelling Ltd is now the second largest company in Cobham plc, after FR Aviation, and is based at Hurn Airport, Bournemouth.

Victories in the Falklands and in the Gulf War owed much to Sir Alan's persistence in pursuing his own ideas to a successful conclusion.

CHAPTER 8

SIDNEY COTTON
CONFLICTS WITH THE BUREAUCRATS

Sidney Cotton's ability to obtain excellent aerial photographs of enemy targets contributed greatly to victory in the second World War. But the jealousy and resentment of those in authority over him finally drove him out of the R.A.F.

Born in Queensland in 1894 Cotton became interested in aviation whilst still at school. Resisting his father's wishes that he should work on the family cattle station he sailed to England in 1916 and joined the Royal Naval Air Service. He was an apt pupil, speedily going solo on a Farman Longhorn. With five hours in his log book he progressed to BE.2s, Breguet biplanes and Sopwith Strutters. Stationed 50 miles from the German and Swiss borders he took part in bombing operations.

The pilots in their open cockpits suffered severely from the cold. On leave in London Cotton arranged for the drapers Robinson and Cleaver to make a flying suit to his own design. This was the origin of the Sidcot suit which came into general use. Indeed Baron Von Richthofen was wearing one when he was shot down.

Cotton shared with another Queenslander, Don Bennett, later to command the R.A.F.'s Pathfinder force, a reluctance amounting to refusal to obey orders that he considered seriously flawed. Stationed at Yarmouth with a special unit of DH.4s his job was to carry out long-range anti-Zeppelin patrols. Finding that the water in the radiator continually boiled away he installed an extra ten-gallon water tank, with a hand pump to top up the contents as the level declined. Without this modification the engine eventually failed.

When one of his officers was ordered to set out for Wilhelmshaven on patrol Cotton appealed to be allowed to conduct the operation himself in the only aircraft fitted with the extra water tank, but this was refused. The unfortunate pilot despatched on patrol suffered precisely the problem Cotton had predicted and had to ditch. He was lucky to be picked up by a naval vessel three days later. Cotton was so enraged that he resigned his commission in order to apply to the newly-formed Australian Flying Corps. But his superiors were unwilling to overlook his insubordination. The Australians were told that he had proved unsuitable and his application was rejected.

The immediate postwar years witnessed attempts by adventurous airmen to make long distance flights. Cotton was anxious to participate. Alcock and Brown had flown the Atlantic ocean but Sir Sefton Brancker loaned Cotton a DH.14A of his Aircraft Manufacturing Company to fly to Australia. Then Keith and Ross Smith reached Darwin, so Cotton attempted a flight to Cape Town. He set off in January 1920 but many problems arose and the endeavour ended on a beach in Sicily, the aircraft turning over on its back.

His next venture was fraught with even more difficulties. He was engaged to fly an aircraft around Newfoundland in order to locate the thousands of seals which appeared on the north shores in March, thence to guide the sealing ships to them. Before very long his employer found himself in severe financial difficulties. The sealers allowed Cotton to take over the contract but his first season as a seal spotter was ruined by mechanical problems with the aircraft. He returned to England, found a financial backer and bought a Martinsyde. Back in Newfoundland in the summer of 1921 he obtained a contract from the government to fly mails, pointing out that winter deliveries occupied dog teams for weeks.

The sealers grew less interested in renewing the contract after Cotton was injured attempting to swing the aircraft propeller. Meanwhile he had learnt to protect the engine from freezing when standing in very low temperatures. Never short of new ideas, he returned to England to see Lord Northcliffe, the newspaper magnate. He suggested that as Newfoundland possessed huge areas of timber in certain parts of the island a proper aerial survey would prove valuable to the paper mills. Northcliffe awarded Cotton a contract and he obtained another from a firm of mapmakers. He also won an order from a Welsh coal mining firm for a quantity of pit props. He engaged a pilot called Hemming, with experience in photography and mapping, to run the aerial survey department.

After three years during which he operated three Westlands and two Martinsydes Cotton decided to liquidate his assets. The pit prop business should have been very profitable but the Welsh firm were so slow to make payments that lengthy legal proceedings ensued. He was particularly exasperated that the local government preferred to pay huge sums to dog teams and local steamship companies to carry the mails, although he could have delivered them far more quickly at half the cost. The reason was political: the government did not wish to lose the votes of the existing organisations.

Cotton believed that the next great industrial development would be in colour photography. Nobody had discovered a satisfactory method of producing colour prints from a negative. He found a firm in Germany that had made greater progress in this field and formed his own company, Dufaycolor.

He continued to travel in his own aircraft and in March 1931 was asked by the chairman of Courtaulds to organise an expedition to Greenland to search for his nephew Augustine, heir to the family fortune. The young man was one of a team of Cambridge undergraduates engaged in an expedition to explore the possibilities of a great circle air route to Canada. Very severe weather had disrupted their plans but Augustine had volunteered to remain on the Arctic icecap for four months. Cotton was put in charge of a combined air and sea search. The youth was spotted, supplies were dropped to him and he was rescued by a ground party.

Cotton was still involved in colour photography in 1938 when Hitler was threatening Czechoslovakia and another war in Europe seemed in prospect. He was asked, through intermediaries, to allow the French to use his private aircraft to photograph German and Italian targets. He was known to fly himself about Europe on business and a British civil aircraft would be less likely to invite suspicion.

Cotton agreed to cooperate but found the task frustrating. He had difficulty persuading the French to allow him to fly the aircraft himself. He was unimpressed by the cumbersome cameras that they had installed and greatly disappointed with the photographs obtained, after the French had finally agreed to let him see them. He returned to England and suggested to British intelligence that better results would be obtained using German Leica film in three of the R.A.F.'s small F.24 cameras. These should be fitted in the fuselage of a Lockheed. When this was agreed he was able to extend the range of the aircraft to 1,600 miles by installing an extra fuel tank.

Cotton was very keen to fly the Lockheed over Germany but was initially ordered to fly out to Aden. En route he was instructed to obtain photographs of Italian installations in Libya, Abyssinia, Eritrea, Rhodes and Sicily. He had a useful "cover" for these flights as he had acquired exclusive sales rights of Dufaycolor cinéfilm in Europe. His journey lasted eleven days and British Intelligence were delighted with the quality of the photographs that he had brought back.

Upon his return the representative of a German company made contact with Cotton. His object was to obtain the agency to market Dufaycolor in Germany. He brought with him an invitation to visit the company in Berlin. On 26th July 1939 Cotton flew the Lockheed to Tempelhof, but without any cameras, certain that the aircraft would be thoroughly searched. He made a return journey to Berlin two days later with his cameras fitted and two loose ones close at hand. He took with him as a passenger C.G. Grey, editor of "The Aeroplane," bound for an air show in Frankfurt.

Cotton invited the commandant of Tempelhof to take a flight in the Lockheed and mentioned that he had been told about the beauty of the Rhine at Mannheim. He would like permission to circle that area. The commandant obtained the necessary clearance and greatly enjoyed the flight whilst 2,000 feet above the Rhine the cameras fitted in the fuselage were busily photographing new airfields and buildings.

Cotton's German business colleagues claimed to be on good terms with Goering. On the spur of the moment he extended an invitation to the Reichsmarshal to accompany him to England as his guest. Back came the reply that Goering would like to fly there on 24th August. Cotton informed Lord Halifax, the Foreign Secretary, and the Prime Minister agreed to entertain Goering at

Chequers. But there was some concern at Cotton's initiative. Ribbentrop, Hitler's foreign minister, was already in Moscow negotiating the Nazi-Soviet Pact. When the news of the signing broke Cotton's business colleagues became worried that the latter would be detained if Hitler sent his troops into Poland.

He shared their anxiety, drove out to Tempelhof and requested clearance to take off for England. He was told that civil flying was banned. Ninety minutes passed and then he was presented with a flight plan to be flown at precisely 1,000 feet. The Lockheed was the last civil aircraft to leave Berlin. As the Dutch border was approached Cotton observed a line of German warships anchored in the Schillig roads outside Wilhelmshaven. These he photographed from the cockpit window with his Leica.

Delighted to receive this information the Admiralty asked Cotton to reconnoitre Heligoland. By this time Germany had invaded Poland but the British government had delayed the expected declaration of war. The Admiralty was alarmed that the German navy would use the interval to send raiders into the Atlantic to prey upon British shipping and asked Cotton to fly over the Wilhelmshaven area once again.

He had bought a Beechcraft with a ceiling of 20,000 feet. His photograph revealed the continued presence of the German ships with the exception of the *"Graf Spee."* The Director General of Operations at the Air Ministry could not understand how Cotton was able to obtain such good photographs whilst the cameras of high-level R.A.F. reconnaissance aircraft always froze. It was explained to him that the cameras did not freeze. The problem was condensation: Cotton had long before learnt how to deal with it.

In the face of the despair of the Admiralty that the R.A.F. could not provide the information that they needed, Cotton asked for a Blenheim to carry out the Wilhelmshaven operation. This request brought the indignant reply that civilians could not possibly expect to fly service aircraft. As arguments and counter-arguments filled the room he left, deciding that he would use his Lockheed for the desired operation. He arranged for Farnborough to be ready to carry out some night-time processing and had Heston tell Fighter Command that he would be engaged on a test flight off the Kent coast.

On his return he showed the photographs to the Director General of Operations and his staff. Their astonishment gave way to indignation at his action. The following day he was summoned to appear before Sir Cyril Newall, Chief of Air Staff. The latter listened intently while Cotton explained how the cameras could be protected against condensation and the method for developing Leica film. He declined Newall's request that he should take charge of the R.A.F.'s photographic department, citing the inevitable resentment that he would incur. However he agreed to form a special unit with his own choice of men and equipment. As Heston had been a civil airport this offered an ideal location for secret operations.

Cotton was accorded the rank of Wing Commander. He obtained the services of five officers already well known to him and 17 technicians. His request for Spitfires was rejected as impossible. He knew that the Blenheims which he was obliged to accept were far too slow for the job. German fighters would make mincemeat of them. Meanwhile he had the thick dope on the Blenheims removed and a smooth surface provided, with other modifications, to reduce drag. This produced an increase in speed of 18 knots.

When Lord Dowding, C. in C. Fighter Command, was informed of this improvement he called at Heston to obtain confirmation. When a flight test proved the reports to be correct he ordered all Blenheim fighter-bombers to be "cottonised." Dowding's pleasure gave Cotton the opportunity to ask for two Spitfires. To the fury of his superiors he got them. He gave their fuselages a hard sleek gloss, had the guns and gun fittings removed and obtained an increase of speed of 30 knots. By fitting a 30-gallon fuel tank under the pilot's seat the Spitfire's range was increased to 1,250 miles.

By October 1939 Cotton had a first-class team that could be expanded and he was ready to undertake operations. But astonishingly the R.A.F.'s own photographic interpretation facility consisted of only two former civilians with virtually no experience of such work. Cotton's solution to the problem was once more to by-pass the "approved channels" and to employ his friend Hemming, still a civilian, who had run his aerial survey department in Newfoundland. But in February 1940 he still had only two Spitfires, although promised eight. The R.A.F. had recently lost 40 Blenheims on photographic reconnaissance. The French had lost 60. In only three flights Cotton's units had photographed twice as many square miles of enemy territory as the R.A.F. without the loss of a single Spitfire.

When Cotton revealed these figures to the Vice-Chief of Air Staff, Sir Richard Peirse, approval was obtained to expand his unit, but little action followed. When the Admiralty asked Cotton to find out whether "*Tirpitz*" was still in dock at Wilhelmshaven, a Spitfire pilot established that it was. To obtain a truly professional identification of the ships and port installations he asked for someone from the Admiralty to be detached to his unit. Back came a direct order from the Air Staff that on no account was he to contact the Admiralty except through Air Ministry channels.

Cotton put the efficient prosecution of the war before service rivalry and delivered a set of desperately-needed photographs to the First Sea Lord, Sir Dudley Pound. In the interview that followed he astonished the admiral with an explanation of the Spitfire's ability to cover a number of targets in the course of one flight. Pound asked Cotton to be present at the confrontation with Peirse that the Admiral had arranged. When the Air Marshal entered the War Room he was unpleasantly surprised to find Cotton there.

According to Cotton's own account Pound expressed his deep dissatisfaction with the failure of the R.A.F. to supply good up-to-date aerial photographs.

When Peirse replied that they were doing their best the First Sea Lord turned to Cotton. "Can your unit obtain this information?"

On receiving an affirmative reply Pound insisted that Cotton should be allowed to tell those present how he would organise the operation. It involved using a Hudson in bad weather in conjunction with the Spitfire. He also urged the requisitioning of Hemming's private firm that had given so much unofficial help to his unit. The Air Ministry had consistently refused to do this. Peirse subsequently offered a better level of cooperation but this took months to achieve.

When the Norwegian campaign was in progress Pound was worried about the possibility of air attacks on British warships, particularly in the Portsmouth area. The Air Ministry had assured him that an excellent early warning system existed. Pound then asked Cotton if he had ever been intercepted during his frequent comings and goings. The latter confessed that he had never been challenged and decided to test the defences. He took off from Heston without filing a flight plan, flew around Portsmouth for 15 minutes and then headed west to Portland before returning to his base. He had his film processed and took the evidence back to the First Sea Lord the next day.

At the subsequent meeting the Air Staff were asked to declare whether there had been any unidentified aircraft over Portsmouth and Portland during the previous day. Pound was told that there was not. When Peirse was shown the photographic evidence he exploded with the one word: "Cotton!"

With his unit in France he had for a time only one Spitfire in operational condition. Blenheims were being flown on reconn-aissance in moonlight but at a heavy cost. Cotton continually begged for two trailers to be supplied so that photographic processing could be speedily done. When he was asked by the Admiralty to submit a dossier of aerial photographs to be shown to the King, Cotton asked to be allowed to interpret these to the Chief of Air Staff who would be presenting them: this was refused.

The next few months culminated in the fall of France whilst Cotton continued to ask for more support from the Air Staff. The C. in C. British Air Forces in France, Sir Arthur Barratt, agreed that the Air Ministry machinery was rusty and cumbersome.

"Go ahead and make your own decisions," he advised. "They will take ages to catch up with you."

He received the same advice from Air Marshal Sholto Douglas. "The R.A.F. is full of regulations made up by people with nothing better to do, which allowed others the chance to delay and sabotage anything they wished."

Cotton continued to try and convince his superiors that photography of important targets should be regular and frequent, not something ordered as a panic measure. He flew home via Jersey, already under attack by German aircraft. A letter from the Air Ministry awaited him; he was ordered to relinquish the command of his unit to a regular serving officer and was posted to the pool depot at Uxbridge. Months passed and no post was offered to him.

When the nightly bombing of London began in the autumn of 1940 Cotton tried to interest the Air Staff in a project to fit a powerful searchlight on night-fighters. This idea was dismissed as impracticable. Never willing to take no for an answer he bypassed senior officers and eventually Lord Beaverbrook, Minister for Aircraft Production, promised him the use of a Boston for trials. The development of the searchlight was undertaken by General Electric. Ultimately Cotton's antagonists prevailed upon Sir Archibald Sinclair, Minister for Air, to block the plan. When he went on to lobby the Prime Minister, Mr Churchill, he was asked to resign his commission.

Cotton's attempt to join the naval air arm was frustrated by the request of the Air Staff that he should not be employed. A ban was placed on him visiting R.A.F. stations. After the liberation of France one of Mr Churchill's personal assistants, on the latter's instructions, booked a flight for Cotton to Paris. He was informed that the Air Ministry had placed a ban on his departure from the country. Churchill personally overturned this order.

Sidney Cotton was courageous and resourceful. Unconventional and self-reliant, his independent character distanced him from colleagues who were content to conform with the practices and mores of a hierarchical society. Such men are often revered by those whom they lead. Sadly they antagonise lesser men set in authority over them.

CHAPTER 9

EDWARD HILLMAN

FROM BUS DRIVER TO AIRLINE BOSS

Not many entrepreneurs can have had a less privileged start in life than Edward Henry Hillman. Born just before the turn of the century he was only two years old when his mother died. At the age of nine he was employed binding brushes. A few years later he joined the Essex Regiment as a bandboy. Transferring to the cavalry he was present at the retreat from Mons and despite a total lack of formal education reached the rank of Sergeant Major. At the war's end he found work as a chauffeur in the diplomatic service. His aptitude as a driver and mechanic won him responsibility for a Rolls Royce: later he was to possess one of his own.

Hillman's ambition was to run his own business. By 1928 he had saved enough money to buy a taxi and at the year's end a motor coach. With this he inaugurated Hillman's Saloon Coaches and opened his first route from Stratford in East London to Chelmsford. Initially he drove the bus himself with his young son as conductor. After a difficult start the business was wildly successful. His coaches carried trippers throughout Essex and beyond to coastal resorts such as Margate and Clacton. He claimed to own about 300 coaches but the real figure was probably much lower.

Hillman paid very low wages to his drivers at a time when the Transport and General Workers Union had insufficient powers to exert pressure on employers. This parsimony enabled him to charge low fares to the public. Then in 1931 the government introduced severe curbs on the unrestricted development of bus operators. Hillman was forced out of business whilst the London Passenger Transport Board absorbed his services. Although he was paid £145,000 in compensation he felt that he had been very harshly treated. Nevertheless with his usual vigour he wasted no time before embarking upon a different form of transport.

In November 1931 he founded Hillman's Airways. He rented a small grass field on sloping ground from a local farmer. This field was near Romford, Essex and he called it Maylands. It possessed a few wooden huts to handle the passengers. Hillman began by purchasing a de Havilland Puss Moth and on Christmas Day his first passenger was carried on a chartered flight. He had engaged a former sergeant pilot, Harold Wood, whom he paid a few shillings more than his bus drivers. He regarded pilots in the same category as bus drivers but with the advantage that they were able to perform work which was very enjoyable to them.

Hillman aimed to fill his aeroplanes with the sort of passenger who had travelled on his coaches but at prices that a working man could afford. This meant cutting costs to the bone. He was a short stout man with a permanent scowl on his rugged face. Very occasionally he was seen in a blue serge suit but more commonly in shirt sleeves with an unbuttoned waistcoat. As the business expanded his preference was to engage as pilots former NCOs rather than officers. "I don't want no high falutin' cocky pilots," he would say.

Those who remained in his service came to realise that his bark was worse than his bite and that he respected those who stood up to him. There was always a furious argument when he was told that the weather was too bad for flying.

The Puss Moth had seats for three occupants in an enclosed cabin but before long Hillman wanted something larger. In March 1932 he visited Stag Lane, then the headquarters of de Havilland, to view their new Fox Moth. He wanted an aircraft with good fuel economy. On arrival he found himself in the company of the Director of Civil Aviation, Colonel Shelmerdine, Sir Alan Cobham and Sir Nigel Norman, of Airwork. Hillman liked what he saw and ordered four Fox Moths.

"It's orl right," he told the bemused salesman. "I can pay for 'em. I got 300 coaches if you want to know."

Each aircraft cost £1,045 and he paid on the spot. By 1st April two were delivered to him and he began a regular scheduled service from Maylands to Clacton.

In September his enterprise was recognised at a ceremony in Romford. The Lord Mayor of London and other dignitaries flew into Maylands in a Spartan Cruiser with an R.A.F. escort of five Westland Wapitis and three Bristol Bulldogs. Other guests arrived at Maylands in private aeroplanes. Hillman's coaches conveyed them all to a reception at the White Hart Hotel. There were speeches and toasts. Hillman began to recite a speech that had originated with Horatio Bottomley.

"I have not had the advantage of education which you enjoy. Mine was the great university of life . . . " Then he interrupted himself: "Oh hell! I can't go on with that rubbish. I just wish you all good 'ealth."

The Fox Moths performed well and the business continued to flourish. Hillman let it be known that he wanted an aircraft twice as large but requiring only one pilot. De Havilland had started work on the DH.84 Dragon, powered by two Gipsy Major engines with seats for six passengers or eight without luggage. The price was below that of its nearest rival, the Airspeed Ferry, designed for Sir Alan Cobham's Circus. The time from drawing board to first flight was four weeks. Hillman was very enthusiastic, declaring the DH.84 to be "just the job, no frills or lah-de-dahs. I am going to run it to Paris like a bus service, you'll see."

He ordered five with a penalty clause that delivery must be in time to open his new cross-Channel service in April 1933.

The price of the DH.84 was £2,800 ex-works; there was a further charge of £150 for six seats. Oil pressure and RPM gauges were positioned on the engine cowlings, clearly visible to the pilot. Scrutinising his bill with great care Hillman exploded at the inclusion of one item.

"They've charged me fifty quid for a shithouse! Fifty quid for a bleedin' shithouse!"

Despite this he was delighted to receive the first DH.84 in December 1932. The famous aviator Amy Johnson was present to break a bottle of champagne over G-ACAN and to christen it "Maylands." The aircraft operated with 100% reliability, the engines delivering 19 gross ton-miles per gallon, a distinct improvement on the Fox Moth. The DH Dragons left Stag Lane to customers worldwide at the rate of one a week. Hillman liked to declare that they were designed to his own specifications although in the first instance the requirements of the Iraqi air force were foremost on the manufacturer's mind.

It was Hillman's ambition to compete with Imperial Airways whose huge Handley Page 42s flew to Paris so slowly that the uniformed stewards served a five-course meal before arrival. Their lowest return fare was £9.18s: Hillman's return fare was £5.10s. No meals were served and the only crew member, the pilot, was indistinguishable in appearance from a bus driver. Flights to Clacton took 30 minutes and to Margate 45 minutes. The return fare was £1 and this included the coach ride to Maylands from Romford bus station. Sometimes almost 50 people waited for a flight. With the DH.84 Hillman had proved the practicability of unsubsidised air transport.

As more pilots were engaged Hillman accepted former R.A.F. officers and appointed W. Anderson D.S.O. as chief pilot. Another, J. Lock, who was later to fly for Imperial Airways, described in his book, *"The Log of a Merchant Airman,"* his experiences working in the company. Pilots were paid £5 a week plus £1 an hour for night flying.

One evening after a long day at the controls Hillman met him with a steaming mug of tea. "Here you are, mate. I reckon you deserve this."

His real purpose was to detain Lock while a further couple of passengers were hurried on board. Hillman invariably disputed pilot's estimates of their time flown in darkness and was not easily convinced by reference to the light-up times printed in the newspapers. The work included plenty of charter flights, particularly at the behest of national newspapers. Pilots were encouraged to seek passengers before returning to Maylands with an empty aircraft.

Railway Air Services, owned by the Big Four railway companies, also bought DH.84s for their internal services. Hillman had only just introduced a service to the north of the British Isles in July 1934 when R.A.S. obtained a mail contract from the G.P.O. and entered into competition. Hillman suspended his own service but increased his Paris service to three flights daily. Before the end of the year he too had won a mail contract and re-installed his service to Liverpool, Belfast and Glasgow.

The first flight of the DH.89 Dragon Rapide, powered by two Gipsy Six engines, took place at Stag Lane in mid-January 1934 and received its certificate of airworthiness by the end of that month. Cruising at about 135 mph it seated up to eight passengers with an endurance of four hours. Once more Hillman was the first customer to put it into service.

On the last day of 1934 Edward Hillman died from a coronary attack. He suffered from high blood pressure and was overweight. His doctor had repeatedly warned him that he was shortening his life through working long hours every day of the week. Yet it had been in his nature to try and make his airline an ever more formidable competitor. Shortly before he died Hillman's Airways had become a public company. All the shares were taken up very rapidly. But Hillman's executors had to sell his own shares on behalf of the family.

Hillman's Airways finally disappeared in December 1935. By that time control had passed to Whitehall Securities. This organisation had swallowed up other internal airlines and was to create the first British Airways. There was not to be another entrepreneur like Edward Hillman for a further fifty years when Freddie Laker appeared on the scene.

"The Times" reported his death as follows:

"Mr Edward Henry Hillman, managing director of Hillman's Airways Limited, and the former motor-coach proprietor, died suddenly at his home in Gidea Park, Essex yesterday, aged about 45. He had been suffering from high blood pressure. Mrs Hillman is ill, but has been told of her husband's death.

At one time in humble circumstances, Mr Hillman rose to become one of the most important operators in Great Britain. He was the pioneer in the country of inland airways, and he later extended his services to Le Touquet and Paris. . .

. . . It was as a motor-coach proprietor that Mr Hillman built up the substantial foundations of the large business he controlled at the time of his death. They grew from very small and hazardous beginnings. Mr Hillman bought his first coach in 1928, and with himself as driver and his son as conductor ran a service between Romford and Chelmsford. It was at first far from successful, and on occasions it was necessary to borrow money to buy petrol. But at last success came to him. In time he was able to acquire more and more coaches until, by the beginning of 1930, he owned a fleet of over 200 and operated extensive services between London, Romford and Chelmsford and along the East Coast.

His enterprise and initiative were unbounded. He was said to be the first motor-coach proprietor to offer penny fare stages and to include motor-coach season tickets between the city and the suburbs. He was quick to see the potential of air travel and then turned his attention to it . . ."

PART 2

THE VENTURERS

CHAPTER 10

THE SOUTH ATLANTIC PIONEERS

The impetus to aviation resulting from military requirements during the first World War inspired efforts to create air links across national boundaries and continents when peace returned. Great Britain was South America's principal European trading partner and half a dozen shipping companies ran cargo and passenger services to that continent. Sadly very little interest in developing an air service was forthcoming.

The first east-to-west crossing of the South Atlantic was made by two Portuguese airmen in 1922. Flying a Fairey IIID seaplane from Lisbon they landed first at Las Palmas in the Canary Islands before continuing to St. Vincent in the Cape Verde Islands and the tiny St. Paul Island, which is just a collection of rocks in the middle of the South Atlantic. There a Portuguese cruiser awaited them. Approaching the island the seaplane ran out of fuel and on touch-down was damaged beyond repair. The two airmen were picked up uninjured and a second, then a third, seaplane was shipped out to them as further mishaps dogged their endeavour. Eventually they completed their flight to Rio de Janeiro.

Before long the commercial possibilities were exploited. A Frenchman, Pierre Latécoère, was far-sighted. He realised that a few years had to pass before an aircraft could be developed to fly non-stop between the French colony of Senegal and Brazil; that sector would remain dependent upon the sea link. But aircraft could be flown to Senegal and the South American republics might be persuaded to allow a French company to operate an air mail service between Natal in Brazil and Argentina. In 1924 Latécoère sailed to Rio de Janeiro, with an aircraft in the ship's hold, to begin negotiations. The aircraft was assembled and he flew on to Buenos Aires.

In June the following year Latécoère instituted a regular mail service from Toulouse to Dakar in Senegal. Initially the aircraft type used was a wartime vintage Breguet XIV, its wooden propeller driven by a 300 horsepower Renault engine. Cruising at 75 mph its range was 435 miles. The route to Dakar was pioneered by Jean Mermoz. On one occasion he was forced to land in the desert. Seized by local tribesmen, several weeks passed before he was released on payment of a ransom.

Another pilot who joined the airline in 1926 is now best remembered as the author of *"Wind, Sand and Stars"* and *"The Little Prince."* This was Antoine de St. Exupéry. For a few months he flew on the sector from Toulouse to Casablanca before being posted to Cape Juby as airport manager. Juby lay in Spanish territory and an important part of St. Exupéry's duties was to search for and rescue airmen who had made forced landings in the desert. The publicity generated by his activities was a source of considerable irritation to the Spanish governor who resented the presence of the French airmen and whose fortified encampment was surrounded on all sides by dissident tribesmen. St. Exupéry's great skill as a diplomat was rewarded when he rescued a Spanish pilot whilst his efforts to establish a working relationship with the tribal chiefs was largely successful.

By the end of 1927 the French were also operating an air mail service between Natal and Buenos Aires but no airports existed between these two places, so landings sometimes had to be made along the coast. Latécoère ran into financial difficulties and sold out to Aeropostale. Jean Mermoz was appointed chief pilot and flew a Laté 26 across the South Atlantic. Regular South Atlantic crossings only began in 1930 when Mermoz and two crewmen flew a Laté 28, fitted with floats, from St. Louis du Senegal to Pernambuco in 21 hours 10 minutes. Thence the mail was flown south to Buenos Aires. The rapid delivery of mail from Europe encouraged other South American republics to invite Aeropostale to inaugurate services to their countries.

St. Exupéry had been 18 months at Cape Juby when he was sent to join Mermoz in Buenos Aires. During his time in Africa 14 aircraft had come down in the desert and six crews had to be ransomed; a few had been murdered. His new job was to extend the airline's routes to Commodoro Rivadavia and Tierra del Fuego in the southernmost part of the continent. By the beginning of 1931

Aeropostale was serving Chile, Peru, Bolivia and Paraguay in addition to Brazil.

Whereas the problems faced by pilots flying south in Argentina sometimes involved wind strengths in excess of the aircraft's own true airspeed, the route from Buenos Aires to Santiago, Chile, required an ability to cross the Andes range of mountains of which Aconcagua at almost 24,000 feet is the tallest. Mermoz was presented with the task of finding a route through the valleys. His aircraft's absolute ceiling was 16,000 feet without provision of oxygen. He discovered a route through connecting valleys but it was only possible to fly through in almost cloudless conditions. At other times when the cloud tops towered above the mountains a pilot faced disaster as his aircraft was buffeted by violent up- and down-draughts and crippled by ice formation. His colleague, Guillamet, fell into the trap; emerging below the cloud base over Laguna Diamante above which the volcano Maipú rises to over 17,000 feet he made a crash landing on the lakeside. He was found a week later, severely frostbitten.

Germany was the next European country to compete with the French for air routes to and within South America. Luft Hansa made use of a catapult ship, "Westfalen," cruising about 950 miles to the West of Bathurst, Gambia. Mail was carried from Germany in a Heinkel He.70 via Stuttgart and Marseille to Seville, thence by Junkers Ju.52 which refuelled at Las Palmas en route to Bathurst. The mail was transferred again to a Dornier Wal seaplane which used a radio direction finder to home in on "Westfalen." After landing alongside the vessel the seaplane was hoisted aboard. Once refuelling was complete it was catapulted off, the pilot setting course for Natal. This service was established on a regular basis in 1933 following many trials. Subsequently, by having a second seaplane already in position on "Westfalen," the mail was transferred and the ocean crossing time was reduced to 14 hours. At Natal a Junkers W-34 seaplane continued the journey to Rio de Janeiro and thence to Buenos Aires. In 1934 Luft Hansa made 47 scheduled flights to South America.

The "Graf Zeppelin" airship service was even more successful than this. In 1932 and 1933 nine flights were made to Rio de

Janeiro and there were twelve in 1934, when 920 passengers were carried along with 3,100 lbs of cargo and mail.

In 1933 Aeropostale fell victim to the worldwide financial depression and went into liquidation. The company was absorbed by Air France which withdrew from all of South America with the exception of the Paris-Buenos Aires route. This left Luft Hansa and Panagra, a subsidiary of Pan American Airways, to share the remaining routes. The Junkers Ju.52 and the Ford Trimotor, used by the Americans before the advent of the Lockheed Electra and Douglas transports, became a familiar sight. In 1936 Air France introduced the Laté 300 flying boat on the route to South America. Other aircraft employed were the Farman F.220, Blériot 5190 and a Laté 301. It was also the year when Mermoz lost his life. Five years earlier he had been rescued when he ditched alongside a steamship in mid-Atlantic; this time his good fortune was not repeated. His last wireless message reported that he was shutting down an engine. But Air France could claim that 86 successful non-stop crossings of the South Atlantic had been completed during the year.

Why therefore was this route neglected by the British? One reason was the condition forced upon Imperial Airways when it became the government's "chosen instrument" in 1924, a private company with shareholders, but dependent upon state grants. The condition was that both aircraft and engines must be of British manufacture and the airline's priority was to serve Europe and the Empire. A further reason was the belated recognition of the military threat posed by Hitler's Germany. By 1936 British aircraft manufacturers had their hands full with orders for the R.A.F. and a very low priority was accorded to civil requirements.

Happily the first European airline to reopen the route to South America after the war was British South American Airways, whose chief executive, Air Vice Marshal Don Bennett, was the former leader of the R.A.F.'s Pathfinder force. The only suitable British aircraft was the Lancastrian, a converted bomber with seats for 13 passengers.

"The Times" of January 2nd 1946 reported the departure of the flight as follows; it was something of a historic occasion, after all, and for more than one reason:

"Lord Winster, Minister of Civil Aviation, Mr Ivor Thomas, M.P., Parliamentary Secretary, and Sir William Hildred, Director-General of Civil Aviation, were among the big crowd at Heathrow, the new London Airport now under construction near Hounslow, to see the first civil aeroplane take off from the 3,000-yard main runway today. The aircraft was the Lancastrian *"Star Light,"* which is making the first of a series of proving flights in preparation for a new service to Buenos Aires.

Captained by Air Vice Marshal D.C.T. Bennett, former head of the R.A.F. Pathfinder Force, the Lancastrian is travelling via Lisbon, Bathurst, Natal (Brazil), Rio de Janeiro, and Montevideo, carring a crew of eight and ten passengers, including officials of British South American Airways, who are to operate the service. It also carried copies of today's edition of *"The Times"* for delivery to the British Ambassadors in the various countries at which refuelling stops are to be made, to the Governor at Bathurst, and to the editors of 16 South American newspapers.

Lord Winster, wishing the passengers and crew bon voyage, said that the Lacastrian was taking off from the finest runway in the world . . . "

B.S.A.A. was also the first airline to fly across the Andes mountains at levels of 25,000 feet or more. But in 1947 a pilot en route to Santiago failed to keep clear of the rising clouds above the mountains. Like the Frenchman Guillamet so many years earlier his aircraft was undoubtedly racked by turbulence, burdened by ice and sucked down to crash into the *cordillera*. To this day the wreckage has never been found. By 1949 pressurised four-engined airliners, invariably Douglas DC-6s and Lockheed Constellations, operated by a number of European countries, routinely visited almost all of the South American republics. B.S.A.A. was absorbed by British Overseas Airways and flew the route with Canadair 4 aircraft, pressurised Douglas DC-4s with Rolls Royce Merlin engines. Thereafter Comet 4s and the Vickers VC-10 plied a route which was abandoned more than once.

CHAPTER 11

CAPTAIN GORDON STORE

FROM PUSS MOTHS TO THE BIG JETS

When Captain Gordon Store made his final landing in a Boeing 707 of B.O.A.C. in 1964 a remarkable career that had begun in 1926 came to an end. Born in Kimberley, South Africa, he had travelled to England to learn to fly at de Havilland's aerodrome, Stag Lane. After obtaining his licence he remained there as an instructor. Then in 1931 he was asked to accompany another pilot in a bid to beat the record time to Cape Town, set by the late Glen Kidston.

The invitation came not from another experienced airman but from a 20-year-old girl whose wealthy parents had given her a DH Puss Moth; her name was Peggy Salaman.

Store recognised that the major responsibility for conducting the flight would rest upon his shoulders. He would have known that two highly-experienced Imperial Airways pilots, Minchin and Hinchliffe, had both lost their lives when accompanied by their young female sponsors on their own attempts to set up records. Whilst there was not an ocean to cross there were huge tracts of desert with no established weather-reporting facilities. Their Puss Moth was not equipped with a radio.

Nevertheless, after taking Miss Salaman aloft to assess her competence as a pilot, he agreed to make the flight. Their Puss Moth was a standard club machine fitted with an extra fuel tank and a metal propeller. To beat the existing record, achieved in a more powerful Lockheed Vega, it would be necessary to fly both by day and night. Leaving Lympne, Kent, on 30th October 1931 their journey proceeded without major incident and on the fifth day they made their seventh landing at Juba in the Sudan. During their stopover Miss Salaman insisted on buying two lion cubs which were carried on the next stage of their night. Then a mechanical fault developed and as the light began to fail Store looked for a suitable place to land. When he touched down the tailplane suffered some damage from contact with saplings.

Numbers of these had to be removed before a clear area for take-off was obtained. Store rectified the mechanical fault but an argument ensued over the future choice of route. He had been born in Kimberley and was determined to land there before concluding the flight to Cape Town. He also wished to offload the lion cubs which had proved to be troublesome passengers. He had his way and the lion cubs were left at Kimberley, eventually accompanying their owner by sea to England. Any ill-feeling over this decision was dissipated by their success in setting up a new record. They landed at Cape Town on the sixth day of their flight, improving on the previous time by about 24 hours.

Store remained in South Africa flying light aircraft for a local company until April 1934, when he returned to England to join Imperial Airways. He had by then recorded a total of 2,600 hours in his log book. That summer he flew as a co-pilot on the four-engined Handley Page 42s to Paris, Zurich and Basle before being seconded to Railway Air Services to fly twin-engined DH.84 Dragons. In October 1934 he was back on the Imperial Airways international routes and revisited Kimberley on the Armstrong Whitworth Atalanta. In 1935 he was promoted to command.

Soon after the airline had begun to take delivery of 28 Empire flying boats Store passed the conversion course, but it was May 1937 before he operated a service to Durban on *"Cambria."* These "C" class flying boats did not have the range to carry a commercial load across the Atlantic ocean but four were stripped of their furnishings to reduce weight and extra fuel tanks were installed in the fuselage. Trials began with the flying boats being refuelled after take-off from Shannon by Sir Alan Cobham's tanker, an old Harrow. Store was one of the Captains chosen to participate. The outbreak of war interrupted the trials and the Air Ministry commandeered two of the modified aircraft, *"Cabot"* and *"Caribou,"* for long range reconnaissance duties with Coastal Command.

Store was in command of *"Cabot"* and, following the German invasion of Norway, flew an R.A.F. unit into Harstad, the main British base for operations against the Germans. The town had already been bombed and there were air raids while *"Cabot"* lay in the harbour. The following day he flew to Bodo, ten miles south of Narvik, to unload equipment; there they were joined by *"Caribou."*

Store and the captain of *"Caribou"* were ashore when a Heinkel was observed circling the port. The two men rowed back to their aircraft and Store managed to taxy away from his moorings before the Heinkel made its first attack. *"Cabot"* was holed in many places and Store was wounded. He ran the flying boat onto the mud at one end of the harbour. In the course of further attacks both *"Cabot"* and *"Caribou"* were set on fire. Store was flown back to Britain in an R.A.F. Sunderland. The other crew members returned in a destroyer.

The desperate need to bring from California the Lockheed Hudsons that had been ordered for the R.A.F. prompted a decision to risk the losses that might be incurred during the severe winter weather on the North Atlantic. The Hudsons would be flown from Newfoundland to Aldergrove in Ulster. R.A.F. personnel could not be spared so Captains Wilcockson, Bennett and Store, each of whom had participated in the flying boat trials, were sent to hire suitable civilian pilots and wireless operators and to organise the delivery programme. None of the volunteers had navigational experience so Bennett prepared flight plans for each crew and brought the first group of seven Hudsons across the ocean. Store led the third group.

In early 1941 he was in R.A.F. uniform once more flying the Short "G" class *"Golden Hind"* on convoy escort duties. His log book records his return to Canada in May to fly one of the Liberator bombers, converted to carry passengers, that had been acquired by Ferry Command to speed the process by which the Hudson delivery crews were transported back to Newfoundland. From June to January 1942 Store was based in Bermuda in command of the R.A.F. unit there. The twin-engined Catalina flying boats which had been ordered for Coastal Command were routinely ferried to Britain via the island.

Meanwhile B.O.A.C., as Imperial Airways had been renamed, had acquired three Boeing 314A flying boats in order to carry VIPs and other passengers on urgent business to and from North America in more comfortable conditions than those provided by a mattress in the bomb-bay of a Liberator. In February 1942 Store joined the Boeing crews at their base in Baltimore.

In winter the route across the Atlantic was between Belem, Brazil and Bathurst, Gambia. In October, flying *"Berwick,"* Store spotted a lifeboat about 60 miles from the coast of West Africa. Descending to circle the lifeboat 16 survivors were observed on board and a sign – "S.O.S. Water." A pillowcase containing some supplies was dropped near to the lifeboat and was seen to be recovered. A shore station was alerted and the survivors were rescued. Their ship had been torpedoed 27 days earlier en route to Freetown from Malta.

In May 1943 Store was in command of the Boeing *"Bristol"* that brought back from Washington Mr Churchill and his advisers. He remained on these flying boats until September 1945 by which time the war had ended.

A former colleague who had commanded Imperial Airways flying boats and organised the Ferry service of military aircraft from Newfoundland was Air Vice Marshal Don Bennett. When he was appointed Chief Executive of a new airline, British South American Airways, he might have expected to be able to recruit some of his old friends, currently working for B.O.A.C. Pension considerations precluded this but Store accepted the post of Operations Manager.

Bennett engaged his pilots from the R.A.F. They were all intensely loyal and enthusiastic men but possessed no experience of international commercial routes nor any knowledge of civil air traffic control procedures. As Bennett did not propose to include among his crews any specialist navigators the first task of his pilots was to pass the examination for an air navigator's licence, first class. The first group of pilots to be enrolled had commanded Pathfinder squadrons.

Since no British airliner had the range to carry passengers across the South Atlantic ocean it was necessary to depend upon converted Lancaster bombers, with seating for 13 passengers. It was not a difficult task to convert pilots whose experience had been gained on Mosquitos or other military types. Store found it less easy to impress upon his captains the overriding importance of safety.

He was in charge of young men who had been expected to fly in every form of dangerous situation. Suddenly, no longer harassed by anti-aircraft fire or night-fighters, many pilots were tempted to make approaches on airports wreathed in fog or covered by low cloud. At that time instrument landing systems did not exist and Ground Controlled Approach was in its infancy. It was rarely available outside Britain.

Before long B.S.A.A. began to suffer accidents at a rate noticeably above that of its competitors. Bennett certainly acknowledged the importance of safety but he was a superb pilot and navigator. In the past he had made long-distance flights demanding exceptional feats of endurance. His example was not likely to be matched by less-qualified mortals. There were then no statutory flight-time limitations and many captains operating delayed services felt it incumbent upon themselves to fly for an excessive number of hours.

Bennett did not allow Store to publish minimum fuel uplifts for the various sectors flown. He declared this to be an encroachment of the captain's right to make such decisions. Those of us appointed to commands at about the time the Avro Tudor was introduced into service knew how worried Store had become about the accident rate. B.O.A.C. had rejected the Tudor but Bennett had declared it to be 10% better than the Lockheed Constellation and ordered it. Apart from the aircraft's other failings the limit of its range was a recurring nightmare to crews operating from the Azores to Bermuda, then the longest ocean sector being flown by any airline.

Pressurised and therefore designed to cruise above 20,000 feet in order to benefit from the highest true airspeed, frequent failures of the cabin heating system obliged captains to reduce altitude. This not only made it necessary to fly in ice-bearing cloud but also made astronavigation impossible, often for long periods. Sometimes a Tudor arrived at Bermuda over an hour late and with little fuel remaining. There was no alternative airport within range.

The disappearance of a Tudor on its way to Bermuda brought about the dismissal of Bennett. The disappearance of a second Tudor, again without any known cause, ended the existence of

TOP LEFT: Brabazon of Tara.
TOP RIGHT: Harry Hawker.
MIDDLE LEFT: Charles Kingsford Smith.
BOTTOM LEFT: Ray Hinchliffe and the Hon. Elsie Mackay.
BOTTOM RIGHT: Sir Alan Cobham and AVM Don Bennett.
All photos via A.S. Jackson.

TOP: Handley Page 0/400 (a converted bomber) at Cricklewood, 1919. Photo: via Croydon Airport Society.
BOTTOM: DH.9B of A.T. & T.: chartered by KLM for the first Amsterdam to London flight in 1919. Photo: via Croydon Airport Society.

TOP: The Handley Page W.8b, the first postwar civil type to enter service, was operated by Imperial Airways until 1932.
Photo: via Croydon Airport Society.
BOTTOM: Cobham's Harrow refuels the Short Empire flying boat *"Cabot"* over Southampton Water, 1939.
Photo: RAF Museum via A.S. Jackson.

Flown by Capt. Wolley Dod, this DH.66 is refuelled, 1920s style, on its journey east of Cairo, January 1927.
Photo: RAF Museum via A.S. Jackson.

TOP LEFT: Sidney Cotton. Photo: via A.S. Jackson.
TOP RIGHT: The R.101 overflies St. Paul's Cathedral in 1929. Photo: via A.S. Jackson.
MIDDLE LEFT: Freddie Laker. Photo: via Freddie Laker.
BOTTOM LEFT: Capt. Gordon Store. Photo: via A.S. Jackson.
BOTTOM RIGHT: George Woods Humphery (left) on the occasion of his enforced resignation, 1939. Photo: via A.S. Jackson.

TOP: A Dornier Wal seaplane is catapulted from *"Westfalen,"* which refuelled her 950 miles west of Bathurst, the Gambia, for the continued flight to Natal, Brazil. Photo: Lufthansa.

BOTTOM: The KLM DC-2 being towed from the mud after its forced landing during the "Last Great Air Race" in 1933.

Photo: via A.S. Jackson.

TOP: Edward Hillman with his Puss Moth at Maylands in 1932. Photo:
via A.S.Jackson.
BOTTOM: A Short Sunderland of 201 Squadron on Berlin's Havel See
during the airlift. Photo: via A.S. Jackson.

TOP: Gordon Olley hands down the mail from the cockpit of a Westland Wessex.
BOTTOM LEFT: Harold Bamberg, founder of Eagle Aviation.
BOTTOM CENTRE: Capt. Marion Kozubski, founder of Independent Air Transport.
BOTTOM RIGHT: Capt. James Thain, who survived at Munich.
All photos: via A.S. Jackson.

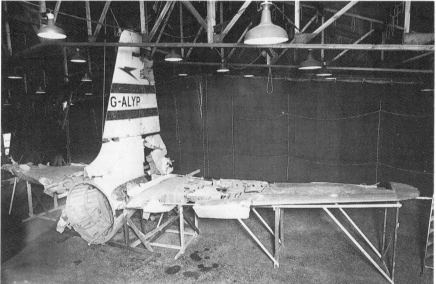

TOP: Inaugural flight of Comet 1 G-ALYP to Johannesburg on the 2nd
May 1952. Photo: via A.S. Jackson.
BOTTOM: The wreckage of the tail unit of G-ALYP at Farnborough after
the accident at Elba.
Photo: RAE Farnborough via A.S. Jackson.

TOP: The naming ceremony on 11th July 1950 of *"Hannibal,"* flagship of the BOAC Hermes fleet, by Chairman Sir Miles Thomas and Lord Pakenham, Minister for Civil Aviation. Photo: via A.S. Jackson.

BOTTOM: One of several mishaps involving the Hermes early in its service life; here the starboard inner propeller and reduction gear broke away, knocking a large hole in the fuselage. Photo: via A.S. Jackson.

TOP: A Tudor 4B, G-AHNM, converted to "Supertrader" standard by Laker's Air Charter Ltd. Photo: via A.S. Jackson.
BOTTOM: The Independent Air Transport Viking G-AIJE, which crashed at Southall on 2nd September 1958. Photo: Peter Davis.

TOP: BEA Ambassador (*"Elizabethan"* class) G-ALZU on the apron at Munich shortly before its last attempted take-off.
BOTTOM: The remains of G-ALZU after the accident.
Photos: via A.S. Jackson.

B.S.A.A. Many of the flight crews, including Store, were absorbed into B.O.A.C.

The senior Corporation was happy to welcome back such an experienced captain and he joined the Boeing Stratocruiser fleet which had replaced the flying boats on the North Atlantic route. In 1956 the delay in delivery of the Bristol Britannias obliged B.O.A.C. to order ten Douglas DC-7s and Store was made manager of this fleet. The following year he flew the Queen and Prince Philip to Ottawa for their royal tour, bringing them home from New York at its conclusion. When B.O.A.C. introduced the Boeing 707 on the North Atlantic service he was among the first captains to make the change to jets and in 1962 flew Prime Minister Macmillan to New York.

Store made his last flight in command of a Boeing 707 in March 1964. He ranked as the second most senior captain in B.O.A.C. In addition to the King's Commendation of Valuable Service, in recognition of his exploits during the war years, his awards included the M.V.O. and O.B.E. His log book recorded a total of over 20,000 hours on 14 four-engined types of aircraft, 8 twins and 15 single-engined aircraft.

As air travel becomes ever more humdrum it is difficult to imagine any future airline pilot whose career will encompass such a wide range of experience.

CHAPTER 12

THE LAST GREAT AIR RACE

In 1933 the Mayor of Melbourne called for an air race from England to commemorate the founding of the city in 1834. He had become concerned at the isolation of Australia, a vast continent with a small population, at a time when the world had barely begun to recover from the economic blizzard that had followed the Wall Street Crash of 1929. Moreover the Japanese government had become the pawn of an aggressive and expansionist military clique. The Mayor's aim was to focus world attention on Australia and thereby to revive the economy.

This idea was taken up with enthusiasm by Sir William Macpherson Robertson, the son of Scottish immigrants, who had make a fortune in a confectionery business. Preferring to be known as MacRobertson, he agreed to finance the event and appointed the Air Races Committee of the Royal Aero Club as chief organiser. Entries for the race had to be submitted by 1st June 1934. The race would start on 20th October 1934. Most, but by no means all, of the interest came from within Great Britain so it is important to appreciate the state of aviation at home at that time.

The R.A.F.'s high-speed fighters were Hawker Fury biplanes. The bombers, such as Vickers Virginias and Hawker Harts, were also biplanes. Veterans of the Royal Flying Corps would not have observed much improvement in technology. Within Imperial Airways the slow and stately Handley Page HP.42 served the Empire routes. Variable-pitch propellers, trailing-edge flaps and retractable undercarriages had not been introduced.

Although Adolf Hitler had become Chancellor in Germany he was not seen as a threat to European security. His verbal onslaughts were directed against Russian communism, an antipathy shared by the Western governments. Rearmament was not in prospect and almost without exception British aircraft manufacturers showed no enthusiasm for developing an aircraft to take part in the race.

The Managing Director of Short Brothers said: "If commercial airline operators call for an aircraft in which the primary purpose is a very high cruising speed and other desires are of secondary importance the demand can be met by British aircraft constructors. There has been no such demand."

Mr Handley Page remarked that low landing speeds were far more important as essential adjuncts to safety.

The exception was Geoffrey de Havilland who declared that it would be intolerable if no British effort was made to win the race. He realised that the most any buyer would be prepared to pay for a racer would be £5,000 whilst the development costs could reach £50,000. However, that expense would be worthwhile if attention was attracted to his company's ability to design a modern aircraft. An advertisement was placed in several aviation journals inviting orders for a racer that de Havilland proposed to build at their works in Stag Lane. The DH.88, to be known as the Comet, would be powered by Gipsy Six engines, would exceed 200 mph and tackle stage lengths of up to 2,600 miles. Construction would be substantially of wood. It would be the first British aircraft to have variable-pitch propellers, a retractable undercarriage and trailing wing flaps. Delivery was promised in the month before the race.

The first order came from Jim and Amy Mollison. In 1930, as Amy Johnson, the latter had flown to Darwin in a Gipsy Moth with less than 100 hours in her log book. Jim Mollison had made a record flight to Australia in 1931 so the Race Committee decided to use his route for the event. He had broken the record of C.W.A. Scott, who was also anxious to enter the race, but required a sponsor. Both these airmen had served in the R.A.F. and each had left the service ahead of their five-year commitments, following repeated breaches of discipline. Both had worked for a short time for Australian airlines and each disliked the other intensely.

Scott teamed up with Tom Campbell-Black, a pilot who had flown during the war. They found a sponsor in the Managing Director of the Grosvenor House Hotel who ordered a Comet which bore the name of the Hotel. The Mollisons had resided for long periods there but their noisy domestic brawls following Jim's drinking bouts did not suggest that they would make good partners in the air.

The third and last Comet to be entered for the race was bought by Bernard Rubin, a wealthy Australian whose family owned sheep stations. He selected Owen Cathcart-Jones as first pilot, along with Ken Waller. Cathcart-Jones, a former Royal Navy pilot, had flown a Lockheed Vega to Cape Town in 1931.

Over sixty other aircraft were entered for the race as aspiring pilots sought sponsors. Most were unsuccessful but some very interesting candidates emerged. K.L.M. Royal Dutch Airlines had acquired their first Douglas DC-2, forerunner of the very successful DC-3 (Dakota). It was not that company's aim to treat the enterprise as a race but to prove the aircraft as a reliable transport carrier over their route to the Dutch East Indies. Pilots Parmentier and Moll, along with a navigator and wireless operator, would be accompanied by several passengers and a load of air mail.

From America came a privately-owned Boeing 247 twin-engine monoplane airliner, a type already in passenger service with United Airlines. The pilots were Roscoe Turner, a former lion tamer, and Clyde Pangborn. Like the Douglas DC-2 this aircraft was equipped with radio and modern technological improvements. The appearance of these two machines opened the eyes of British observers to the obsolescence of the airliners operated by Imperial Airways. Others entered included K.L.M.'s tri-motor Pander, a Lockheed Vega whose navigator was a youthful D.C.T. Bennett (of subsequent R.A.F. Pathfinder fame), a Granville Gee Bee flown by an American woman, Jacqueline Cochran, and a Fairey Fox purchased for £200 by Ray Parer. He had participated in the 1919 air race to Australia which had been won by Keith and Ross Smith in a Vickers Vimy.

Whilst de Havilland was building the three Comets the race organisers were drawing up the rules to be observed and a method of handicap for the various types of aircraft. It was decided to have both a speed and handicap section. Contestants could enter both but not receive two prizes. Sir William MacRobertson was offering a Gold Cup to the victorious speed section entrant together with a cheque for £10,000, and smaller sums for the runners up. The winner of the handicap section would receive £2,000.

The Royal Air Force agreed to allow a new grass airfield, under construction at Mildenhall in Suffolk, to be the starting point of the race. The hangars were ready for use and 1,400 yards was available for take-off. No other amenities existed – for lack of a windsock a bonfire was lit and two pillowcases were stitched together and attached to a post. There was no night illumination. Urgent diplomatic efforts had to be made to persuade Turkey to permit landing rights to the contestants. Eventually these were successful although Mollison was excluded from the concession; he had made an unauthorised landing in Turkey in 1931.

The first compulsory en route landing airfield was Baghdad, 2,530 miles from Mildenhall. Thereafter stage lengths decreased to take into account the increasing fatigue of the flyers: Allahabad after a further 2,300 miles, 2,210 miles to Singapore, 2,058 to Darwin, 1,384 to Charleville, 787 to Melbourne. As the start date approached the number of entrants dwindled to 20 aircraft. Among these there was a DH Puss Moth which, like other small machines, could be expected to land at a very great number of airfields. De Havilland was able to hand over the three Comets to their pilots only days before the start date. Each aircraft had only a few hours recorded in its log book. Consequently the pilots had time to practise few landings before the race. The Comet had to be landed on its forward wheels, tail up, as a three-point attitude caused a wing to drop. Once the tail was down the pilot lacked adequate forward visibility, while his companion on the rear seat was completely blind.

The day before the start of the race King George V and Queen Mary visited Mildenhall. The American Roscoe Turner, addressing the monarch as "King," invited the royal couple to board his Boeing. Urged by Queen Mary the King agreed to do so. He disliked the whole concept of aviation and inspected no other machines. There had been great public interest in what the *"Daily Telegraph"* called "the greatest air contest ever held." Extra police had been drafted in to combat souvenir hunters who had tampered with some of the aeroplanes .

At 6.00 am on 20th October 1934 the Mollisons' Comet, named *"Black Magic,"* was flagged off first, the nineteen other aircraft following at 45-second intervals. The Boeing took off next and the

Comet flown by Cathcart-Jones was third off. Carrying the maximum possible fuel each aircraft used most of the available airfield surface. The Mollisons landed at Baghdad 12 hours and 40 minutes after leaving Mildenhall. Immediately their engines were switched off they called out: "Are we the first?" and hearing that this was so decided to make Karachi their next stop rather than a direct flight to Allahabad. This added 180 miles to the total route distance but would ensure that they broke Mollison's own England to India record.

Ten minutes after their departure the Comet of Scott and Campbell-Black was observed on the approach. They had already made one landing, at the R.A.F. station at Kirkuk, 130 miles north of Baghdad, after becoming lost in bad weather over Assyria. They were encouraged by the knowledge that the Mollisons were en route to Karachi and hoped to make up time by flying direct to Allahabad. They expected that they could achieve this subject to accurate navigation, but de Havilland had not had time to make accurate fuel consumption tables for varying distances. Within 35 minutes of landing at Baghdad they were on their way.

Cathcart-Jones and Waller unintentionally overflew Baghdad and were lucky to make a safe night-landing in the desert. At dawn they flew west to reach Baghdad. On departure they had to shut down the starboard engine and make their return. When servicing was complete they made for Karachi. When they finally made Allahabad they were three hours behind the Mollisons but had a propeller defect which kept them five hours on the ground.

Meanwhile others had come to grief in the course of the race. Jacqueline Cochran had landed at Bucharest with a jammed trailing-edge flap, damaging her aircraft beyond repair. Later she was to declare that she was the only owner among the six purchasers of the Granville Gee Bee who did not kill herself in one. An Airspeed Envoy flown by Neville Stack and S. Turner retired from the race with engine trouble. A Fairey Fox owned by two Australians crashed at Foggia in Italy, killing both men. The Lockheed Vega navigated by Don Bennett tipped on its back after landing at Aleppo to be out of the race.

The Mollisons landed at Karachi 22 hours 13 minutes after leaving Mildenhall, thereby knocking 28 hours off the existing record. They continued to Allahabad; then they were plagued with problems. After take-off they had to return because the undercarriage would not fully retract. They took off again and returned once more, either because they had left some charts behind or did not possess adequate ones. By this time each was blaming the other for their difficulties. A race official who examined the cockpit observed three empty bottles of spirits beside Mollison's seat. Sixteen hours had been lost. After their next take-off their compasses did not agree, obliging them to land at Jabalpur, 175 miles south east of Allahabad. They were no longer in contention for a prize and abandoned the race.

The DC-2, the Boeing and the Pander were all following Scott and Campbell-Black. The Pander reached Allahabad shortly after the DC-2 but landed with the undercarriage unlocked. After repairs it was taken up for an air test but struck a lighted beacon on the airfield and crashed. When the Boeing reached Allahabad the DC-2 was at Rangoon whilst Scott and Campbell-Black were about to arrive at Singapore. The latter noticed the windsock and shouted a warning to Scott that he was about to land downwind. Fatigue was having its effect.

Their flight to Darwin involved a 900-mile passage over the shark-infested Timor Sea. It was at that stage that the oil pressure of one engine dropped to zero, obliging them to throttle it back. They reached Darwin safely and attended to the engine during the refuelling process. When they reached Charleville they were told that their closest rival, the K.L.M. DC-2, was on the ground at Darwin.

K.L.M. was undoubtedly the most ambitious international air operator and Parmentier and Moll were backed by the superb professional handling of that company's station staff. The two Dutchmen lost their equanimity for the first time when they arrived over Charleville to find the airfield unlit, obliging them to orbit for 45 minutes.

There remained the shortest stage of all, to Melbourne. Night had fallen and there were thunderstorms and vivid flashes of lightning. Radio communication was impossible. Helped by car headlamps and flares they landed at Albury, 190 miles north-east of Melbourne. Coming to a halt the aircraft wheels sank into boggy ground. Over a hundred volunteers manning ropes dragged the aircraft on to drier ground. The passengers and mail were offloaded and the DC-2 took off again to conclude the flight.

Scott and Campbell-Black had already arrived to take the first prize. They had made the journey from Mildenhall in 70 hours 55 minutes. The DC-2 gained second place after a flight of 90 hours, to be followed three hours later by the Boeing. This aircraft had also crossed the Timor Sea with falling oil pressure in one engine and a serious oil leak in the other. Before reaching Melbourne Roscoe Turner had prudently made a precautionary landing at Bourke. Cathcart-Jones and Waller in their Comet were fourth. Altogether 12 aircraft reached the finish on the Flemington racecourse, some of these arriving days later.

What of the victorious pilots? Scott and Campbell-Black received neither the Gold Cup nor the £10,000 prize. These were claimed by their sponsor who had paid for the aircraft. Nor would he allow Campbell-Black to buy it. He preferred to sell it to the Air Ministry for £7,000. The two airmen did receive a generous cheque from Lord Wakefield, whose oil they had used. Any further monetary rewards had to be earned from speaking engagements and contracts with newspapers.

Whilst the centenary celebrations got under way in Melbourne more serious thoughts were occupying the minds of certain agencies in England. There were demands for all-weather aerodromes, concrete runways, radio beacons at regular intervals on the ground and the provision of wireless receivers and transmitters on airliners.

Viscount Hailsham said: "The air race has shown how tremendously the possibility of attack from the air has increased. The English Channel as a frontier defence has disappeared."

The race had also revealed the pre-eminence of American airliners. De Havilland urged the Air Ministry to recognise the fact that European airlines were looking to the United States for commercial aircraft. This trend would be followed by the British Dominions, South America and the Far East. Purchase of military aircraft would follow. The Air Ministry's response was that it could not place a non-competitive order for the construction of a prototype with a single firm.

The performance of K.L.M. was greatly admired. The company declared that when the British government permitted it to do so it planned to run a seven-day service to Australia. Their DC-2 had made 19 landings in the course of the race. Transit times on the ground had varied between 22 and 46 minutes. K.L.M. placed an order for 10 more DC-2s with Douglas.

The slow and obsolescent airliners of Imperial Airways brought the spotlight on that company's future plans. A service to Melbourne occupying 16 days had been announced. The Chairman, Sir Eric Geddes, tried to play down unfortunate comparisons. He said that the DC-2 had not carried a commercial load or it would have had to make twice as many landings to take on fuel. Formalities such as Customs inspections had been waived. He insisted that speed was not all-important. Imperial Airways would continue on its steady, non-spectacular, plodding way, the soundest and best in the end. The Under Secretary of State, Sir Philip Sassoon, did not provide much encouragement for aviation enthusiasts when he declared that Imperial Airways could do no better. The company had to pay dividends to shareholders whereas the United States government paid huge subsidies to their airlines, disguised as mail contracts.

In 1935 Adolf Hitler boasted that in defiance of the Treaty of Versailles the Luftwaffe was larger than the Royal Air Force. Belatedly the British Government began a programme of rearmament. One result was the very low priority accorded to the construction of civil aircraft. But de Havilland built seven DH.91 four-engined airliners in the same manner as their DH.88 Comet, the fuselage with laminations of cedar ply and a layer of balsa wood inbetween. They did not stand up to the rough uneven surface of Croydon Airport. In 1938 the designers began work on a bomber version; the Air Ministry had only been persuaded to order it because de Havilland did not require allocations of scarce metals.

The outcome was the Mosquito, the most versatile of any aircraft that was flown during the second World War.

CHAPTER 13

GEORGE WOODS HUMPHERY

SCAPEGOAT FOR A TROUBLED AIRLINE

In 1924 the British Government reluctantly decided to create Imperial Airways as the nation's flag carrier – the "chosen instrument." The Treasury was not at all favourable to civil aviation but the experience of the few years since the war had shown that the small private companies were at a huge disadvantage in competition with the subsidised Dutch, French and German airlines.

The usual British compromise was cobbled together. Imperial Airways would be a private company with shareholders but the government would support it with a subsidy. Inevitably the opposition Labour party expressed fears that "private finance, private plunder . . . would put its finger in this pie as it had in telegraph and telephones." The terms of the agreement included the stipulation that the airline must operate aircraft of British manufacture. This was to prove a severe handicap in later years when the rearmament programme gave priority to R.A.F. requirements, whilst the Company's competitors bought modern faster aircraft from the United States. In this constitution the seeds of an eventual explosion of discontent against the performance of Imperial Airways were sown.

Sir Eric Geddes, Chairman of the Dunlop Rubber Company, knew nothing about aviation but reluctantly accepted the government's request that he should add the airline to his responsibilities, as part-time Chairman. Several small private companies operating converted bombers merged to form the "chosen instrument." Their owners joined two government appointees as members of the Company's board. The post of general manager was assigned to a former Royal Flying Corps pilot, Major George Woods Humphery.

Woods Humphery's role since joining Handley Page Transport in 1919 had been in management. At the end of 1921 when the British companies could no longer survive against foreign competition he had supported the attempts of Colonel Searle, organiser of the London General Omnibus Company, to form a new airline. Daimler Airway came into being, funded by the BSA-Daimler combine. The Daimler Hire system of intensive utilisation of cars was adopted to aircraft in order to obtain 1,000 hours flying time annually by each one.

Nevertheless the efforts of Daimler to compete against its British rivals Handley Page Transport and Instone, in addition to the European airlines, proved futile. Sir Samuel Hoare was the first Secretary of State for Air to have a seat in the cabinet. It was the cabinet committee whose findings had led to the creation of Imperial Airways.

The Company proposed to engage only 16 pilots, intending to offer the remainder re-employment when business picked up. But even the fortunate ones expressed hostility to the appointment of Woods Humphery as general manager. Those who had flown for Handley Page and Daimler regarded him as a martinet who was impatient with pilots reluctant to fly aircraft which they did not consider free of defects. Many former pilots will recall that an engineer's report of "ground-run and found OK" implied a faultless engine. The pilots claimed the right to decide for themselves whether fog or thunderstorms made it unwise to begin a flight.

The response of Woods Humphery was to serve a writ for libel upon the pilots. These young men, all of whom had served during the war, had been paid between £825 and £1,000 per annum by their former employers. A few days before the new airline was due to commence operations they were offered a salary of £100 a year plus two pence per mile flown, the contract to be terminated at one day's notice. In their fury they accepted the offer of support of two notorious trade union militants, Ben Tillett of the Dock Workers and Bob Williams of the Transport Workers. Both men had tried in 1921 to bring out all their members in support of the miners.

The Air Ministry and other interested parties intervened. Sir Samuel Instone suggested the appointment of an Air Superintendent, someone whose reputation was known and respected by the pilots. Woods Humphery put forward the name of Major Brackley, a wartime pilot recently returned from a military mission to Japan, after a short stint with Handley Page. The pilots agreed and when the issues of salary and conditions of service were resolved Woods Humphery was persuaded to withdraw his writ.

Captain Ray Hinchliffe, who wore a patch over one eye, had flown for K.L.M. as chief pilot before being engaged by Daimler Airway in that capacity. He did not get on with Woods Humphery and had transferred to Instone. On the appointment of Brackley he wrote in his log book: "We considered that the management and general system was dangerous and we hoped that Brackley . . . would carry out his duties fairly otherwise fatal accidents would result."

Imperial Airways began operations with 14 biplanes. Half of these were DH.34 single-engined machines. There were only three airliners built specifically for civil use after the war. These were twin-engined Handley Page W.8B machines which had seats for 14 passengers. The airline's daily schedule to its European destinations called for the availability of six aircraft but sometimes only one or two were serviceable.

The national newspapers seldom gave prominence to aviation except to report accidents or record-breaking attempts. The most reliable authority for the post-1919 period was the founder and editor of "The Aeroplane," C.G. Grey. He had also founded the Royal Aeronautical Society in 1909. He was a stern critic of the shortcomings of Imperial Airways, particularly the Company's failure to provide information on its intentions over the development of routes. Throughout its history the airline's public relations never did justice to its achievements.

Woods Humphery acknowledged this; appointed general manager at the insistence of Colonel Searle he replaced the latter as managing director early in 1925. The Company was losing money and Sir Eric Geddes was unhappy. Woods Humphery and C.G. Grey were on friendly terms and the former made it clear that the Board would not go to the expense of hiring a public relations officer.

Although Major Brackley had been appointed Air Superintendent at the suggestion of Woods Humphery he was threatened with dismissal by the latter in 1926. In a letter he was accused of a lack of foresight, tact and leadership and a failure to take advantage of the talent that existed among the pilots. However he survived a period of probation although ultimately others were ranked in posts above him.

Less fortunate was Lt. Colonel Minchin, the Company's senior ranking pilot, who had participated in the scheme to set up an airmail service to the Middle East. It had been his task to land at every single aerodrome which it might be necessary to use. But in 1927 he was piloting a Handley Page W.9 to Croydon when the fuel ran out and the aircraft was damaged in a forced landing. At that time fuel contents gauges were not only inaccurate but not always easily visible to the pilot. The records show that Minchin was held responsible and dismissed. He lost his life shortly afterwards in an attempt to make the first east-to-west crossing of the North Atlantic.

However tough his style of personnel management might have been, Woods Humphery worked extremely hard. He was generally regarded as deputy to Geddes although this post was nominally occupied by Sir George Beharrel. His duties often took him abroad and he spent seven weeks in Persia trying to persuade the ruler to grant overflying rights for the air service to India and beyond.

Perhaps Sir Samuel Hoare is best remembered for his association with the appeasement policy towards the dictators when he was a member of Mr Chamberlain's government. He was however an enthusiastic supporter of civil aviation and in January 1927 travelled out to India on the first flight of the Company's de Havilland 66. The following year he agreed that the principal task of Imperial Airways should be to concentrate its efforts on routes to the Empire.

At the same time the government gave no encouragement to other British airlines to develop services to Europe. Only the "chosen instrument" was entitled to a subsidy. Imperial Airways abandoned the route to Amsterdam to K.L.M. and allowed the Germans to carry passengers from Croydon to Berlin. Although ultimately the Company's own efforts were devoted almost exclusively to overseas routes, most of its passengers travelled within Europe and criticism of its services increased in volume.

Four years passed before Imperial Airways was able to pay a dividend to its shareholders. By then foreign airlines were so well established that the Company was acting as their ticket agents. However a charter department was formed under Gordon Olley, one of the original 12 pilots, to seek out unscheduled business.

Although priority was being given to routes to the Empire Woods Humphery tried to impress upon the Secretary of State the need for the Air Ministry to develop an airliner capable of crossing the North Atlantic. Vickers then began work on a six-engined flying boat. Woods Humphery followed this up with a trip to New York to meet Juan Trippe, founder of Pan American Airways. At that time it was only possible to have a gentleman's agreement that neither airline would operate to the territory of the other until both were ready to do so. Trippe promptly engaged Colonel Lindbergh to report on the feasibility of the Arctic route.

The problem on the more southerly route was the huge distance between the Azores and Bermuda. Then in 1931, with the world suffering a severe economic depression, Lord Trenchard's determination to retain any small sums voted for the benefit of the R.A.F. resulted in the Air Ministry's cancellation of work on the Vickers flying boat.

In 1932 Imperial Airways initiated an airmail service to Cape Town. The journey took over ten days and five different types of aircraft over the various stages. C.G. Grey frequently recommended Imperial Airways to concentrate on mail to the exclusion of passengers. This was the policy that had been adopted in the United States. He pointed out that the Duchess of Bedford had flown her own aircraft to India and back in one week, the time it took the Company to go one way.

At the end of that year Woods Humphery accompanied Geddes in a Handley Page 42 to South Africa. It provided an opportunity to explain to the Chairman the plan of the company secretary, S.A. Dismore, for Imperial Airways to carry all letter mail throughout the Empire without an air surcharge. This plan required the agreement of the G.P.O. and the Air Ministry with the government paying an economic rate. Geddes was convinced, but it took two more years for the initiative to produce results. Once the necessary agreements were obtained Imperial Airways ordered 28 four-engined flying boats from Short Brothers.

In Europe the Company continued to operate services to Paris, Brussels, Zurich and Cologne. They were not profitable and did not compete in terms of speed. 95 mph was far inferior to that being achieved by the Boeing monoplane with a speed of 150 mph. Within Britain the railway companies, alarmed by competition from coach operators, obtained government permission to run air services and Imperial Airways agreed to provide flight crews and technical support. The railway companies then warned travel agencies, most of whose business was in rail tickets, that they should confine the sale of airline tickets to those of Imperial Airways and foreign airlines. This anti-competitive device was directed against the new domestic airlines which, unsubsidised, were going into business. Their protests caused questions to be asked in Parliament.

Gordon Olley left Railway Air Services to run his own airline. A former coach operator, Edward Hillman, started with one Puss Moth and before long was operating to Paris with a de Havilland Dragon. His fare was lower than that of Imperial Airways and the journey was completed in 30 minutes less time. When Hillman died the banking house of d'Erlanger bought all the shares. Thereafter Hillman Airways was one of five companies swallowed up by Whitehall Securities whose progeny was the first British Airways Ltd, a company in which the government held no financial stake.

This newcomer was under no obligation to operate aircraft manufactured in Britain and purchased Fokkers, Junkers 52s and Lockheed 10s. By 1935 the rearmament programme was keeping British aircraft builders busy with orders for the R.A.F., making it even harder for Imperial Airways to improve their European services. To add to their problems Geddes was told by the Secretary of State for Air, Viscount Swinton, that there was dissatisfaction being expressed within the House of Commons and among the public in regard to the continuing monopoly enjoyed by the Company. He expected that a second British airline would be allowed to fly services to Europe and that it would receive a government subsidy. When Geddes protested that this would make nonsense of the original government agreement of 1924 Swinton replied that no agreement remained irrevocable policy for all time.

Worse was to come. In 1934 Imperial Airways had ordered 14 four-engined Armstrong Whitworth Ensigns, designed to carry 40 passengers at a cruising speed of 200 mph. The original engines failed to deliver the necessary power and there were problems with the airframe. Several more years were to pass before they entered service. The manufacturer was giving top priority to the order for Whitley bombers. De Havilland's DH.91 Albatross was designed and built in 16 months but the undercarriage was too fragile to cope with the undulating grass surface of Croydon and other such airfields. Hopes were entertained that the DH.95 Flamingo, a twin-engined metal monoplane, would be more successful but once again military orders took priority.

In 1937 Sir Eric Geddes died. He was suceeded as Chairman by Sir George Beharrel, who also replaced him at the Dunlop Rubber Company. Thus an enormous load of extra responsibility was laid upon the shoulders of Woods Humphery at the most difficult period in the airline's history. The Board of Imperial Airways had voted an increase in the fees paid to the directors from £6,500 to £12,000 a year. At the next annual general meeting Beharrel announced that the directors were to be rewarded by a further £5,000. A dividend of 7% plus a 2% bonus would be paid to shareholders. Meanwhile the Company's pilots had become increasingly frustrated in their efforts to negotiate pay and conditions. The constitution of the Guild of Air Pilots and Air Navigators to which many of them belonged did not permit it to engage in such matters. This had resulted in the formation of the British Air Line Pilots' Association. Lord Chesham agreed to become President and a Conservative M.P., Robert Perkins, Vice President. The latter flew his own aircraft on business trips to Europe.

The pilots were unhappy about the obsolete aircraft that they were expected to fly. Few of these were equipped to combat ice formation and none were provided with the Standard Beam Approach system for blind landings. A further cause for their concern was the knowledge that new pilots currently being engaged were being offered salaries lower than the existing scale.

The response of Imperial Airways to B.A.L.P.A.'s representations was a refusal to concede their right to collective bargaining.

Neither Woods Humphery nor Brackley were sympathetic to the pilots' case. Both took the view that only the lowest-paid workmen needed to resort to a union and that channels existed within the airline to resolve complaints. Relations become further strained when six pilots were dismissed. Two of these had suggested that the winter service of DH.86 aircraft to Budapest should be suspended as the icing encountered made them unsafe to fly. The Company complied with this suggestion and then dismissed both pilots as surplus to requirements.

Woods Humphery expressed doubts that B.A.L.P.A. truly represented the pilots. Other airlines had not recognised it. In fact 74% of the pilots had become members. However it was true that some of the most senior of the Company's captains such as O.P. Jones had not joined. Others were extremely unhappy about suggestions of a strike. Air Vice Marshal Don Bennett, later of Pathfinder fame, was then a very young but highly-qualified pilot, who was taking part in both the North Atlantic flying boat trials and the *"Mercury-Mayo"* composite programme. He held Woods Humphery in high regard. His opinion on the pilots' tactics, when questioned by the author, was that the leadership of B.A.L.P.A. had been usurped by trouble-makers.

In an editorial in *"The Aeroplane"* C.G. Grey was critical of the failure of Imperial Airways to recognise B.A.L.P.A. He thought it inevitable that the pilots would wish to organise for their own protection when so many companies were amalgamating into a single large airline. In addition he criticised the increased dividends being paid to shareholders. Government bonds were paying 2¼%. As the Company's dividend was being paid from public funds it should be no higher than that.

On 28th October 1937 Robert Perkins had an opportunity to tell the House of Commons why there was so much discontent among the pilots. He mentioned the reduction in the salary scale at a time when the fees of the directors were being increased. He questioned the reasons for the dismissal of six pilots. He deplored the failure to provide blind-flying equipment and devices to combat ice formation. He declared the Company's services within Europe to be "the laughing stock of the world."

In the course of a debate on civil aviation on 17th November Perkins returned to the attack, disputing statements in the newspapers that pilots were paid £1,500 per annum: some captains received only £300. He drew attention to the Company's safety record. There had been two major accidents within the last two years involving loss of life. In nine other accidents only amazing good luck had prevented further fatalities when some aircraft had been completely destroyed. He revealed that the fuel capacity on some flying boats was inadequate for the stage lengths being flown. More than once aircraft had landed with their fuel tanks almost empty.

Lieut. Colonel Moore Brabazon (later Lord Brabazon of Tara) supported Perkins, telling the House of Commons that in America airliners currently incorporated variable-pitch propellers, flaps and retractable undercarriages. These improvements had added 100 mph to their speed.

It was unfortunate for Woods Humphery that the wide-ranging criticisms by Perkins on the state of British civil aviation were interpreted by many listeners as criticisms of his own management. He himself did not need reminding of the dependence of Imperial Airways on the support and goodwill of the Air Ministry. He considered that this had consistently been far below the desired standard.

The object of Perkins' campaign was to force the government to institute a Committee of Enquiry. He was successful and a Committee, headed by Lord Cadman, was given wide terms of reference and began interviewing witnesses *in camera*. Imperial Airways was never shown any of this evidence so could not refute specific charges. As regards the need for a faster aircraft on European routes the Company had found it impossible to come to an agreement with the Air Ministry to justify the cost of an airliner seating 16 passengers. The American Goodrich deicer was not considered efficient. Imperial Airways proposed to smear "Killfrost" paste on the leading edges of the wings and tailplane. Hardly any airports in England were provided with the Standard Beam Approach so there was no hurry to install the airliners with receivers. Imperial Airways earned the greater part of its revenue from services to the Empire which accounted for 90% of its route mileage. Its network embraced Australia and the Far East as well as Africa, the most extensive of any airline in the world.

During the summer of 1937 Sir John Reith, Director General of the B.B.C., informed the government that he would like to take on an additional appointment. In no way did he have Imperial Airways in mind. For one thing he and Woods Humphery had once worked in the same firm as apprentices and he had been best man at the latter's wedding. They had kept up their acquaintance, meeting for lunch from time to time, comparing their two organisations. On one such occasion Reith had expressed the view that Imperial Airways had too few senior managers and that these were underpaid. He suggested that the airline had a serious need for a top-grade public relations officer and added that he thought the dividend motive to be too predominant.

Woods Humphery reminded Reith that Imperial Airways did not have the financial resources of the B.B.C., a public Corporation. As to dividends its first duty was to the shareholders. He expressed no support for Reith's view that the public service aspect should take precedence. They met again in November 1937 when rumour had it that Reith would be replacing Beharrel as Chairman, and not in a part-time capacity. Woods Humphery was insistent that there was not enough for a full-time chairman to do.

In March 1938 Lord Cadman's Report was published. That part of it which caused the greatest stir was the Committee's criticism of Woods Humphery.

"We cannot avoid the conclusion that the management has been defective. Not only has it failed to cooperate fully with the Air Ministry but it has been intolerant of suggestion and unyielding in negotiation. Internally its attitude in staff matters has left much to be desired. It appears to us that the Managing Director . . . has taken a commercial view of his responsibilities that was too narrow."

Charging Woods Humphery for failing to cooperate with government departments the Report pointedly recommended "some change in directing personnel." Finally it urged the

Chairman to give his whole time to the direction of the Company in preference to reliance upon a Managing Director.

The Cadman Report covered a very great number of matters. C.G. Grey declared it to be the most sensible document that had ever been issued on civil aviation. But he remained steadfast in support of Woods Humphery whom he thought to be the obvious choice as Chairman. He added: "The great thing is take some of the work off his shoulders. But quite definitely his resignation would be the very worst thing that could happen."

The spokesman for the Captains' Committee of Imperial Airways declared their unanimous satisfaction with Woods Humphery and expressed their approval that he had been "intolerant of suggestion and unyielding in negotiation" with the Air Ministry.

Reith had let it be known that he was most reluctant to go to Imperial Airways and put his old friend out of a job, but he assumed that the sharp criticism that he had suffered would oblige Woods Humphery to offer his resignation, or be asked to do so. But he was mistaken; with the support of Beharrel and most of the Board the Managing Director declared that his sense of responsibility to the shareholders would not permit him to resign.

Reith now found himself under great pressure to accept the chairmanship, particularly as the government had offered it to two others who had declined the opportunity. When Mr Chamberlain personally asked him to accept Reith felt bound to comply. The Prime Minister's closest adviser, Sir Horace Wilson, told him to insist upon the resignation of Woods Humphery. So too did Sir Warren Fisher, Permanent Secretary to the Treasury, and Sir Montagu Norman, Governor of the Bank of England. Norman also recommended the transformation of the Company into a public corporation, an action which Reith fully supported.

Woods Humphery finally submitted his resignation when Reith told him that if he wished to remain as General Manager he would not be permitted to continue as a member of the Board.

The staff of the Company closed ranks in support of their beleaguered chief. From 111 stations cables representing 3,600 employees deplored his resignation. At a testimonial dinner their gift of a silver salver was presented to Woods Humphery. In his speech Captain Wilcockson spoke of "a dirty political move." From

Australia Hudson Fysh, Chairman of Qantas, cabled: "Resignation Woods Humphery at this stage inauguration Empire air services fantastic and unacceptable. Do hope British stability will prevail."

C.G. Grey suspected that the government wanted Woods Humphery removed because "he was the effigy and victim of Sir Eric Geddes." Grey considered Geddes to have been a dictator without an intimate personal touch.

"The Observer" commented: "Mr Woods Humphery was charged with making commercial aviation pay and he came nearer to succeeding than anyone else in the world. Sir John Reith is charged with making British aviation technically advanced, no matter whether it pays or not."

A major cause of the Company's problems was its dependence upon the Air Ministry. The Handley Page Harrow which had gone into production for the R.A.F. in 1935 was obsolete as soon as it appeared, not remotely comparable to current American transports. The Air Ministry was reluctant to devote funds to an aircraft which the Army might require for troop movements. Their civil servants were accountable to the Treasury and lacked experience in commercial considerations. Preoccupation with short-stage operation on the Empire routes left the Company without an airliner suitable for passenger carriage across the Atlantic ocean.

Woods Humphery knew better than anybody else those in government who had obstructed the airline's progress. If he had been appointed Chairman he would have been a far greater thorn in their flesh than Sir Eric Geddes had ever been.

Was he made the scapegoat for the Company's problems? A few years ago the author put this question to Air Vice Marshal Bennett and to Air Commodore Powell – the latter had also been a senior Imperial Airways captain. Neither hesitated before agreeing that such had been his fate.

CHAPTER 14

THE EMPIRE FLYING BOATS
IN WARTIME

In 1939 Great Britain possessed an airline network covering Africa, the Middle East and Australasia. Built by Short Brothers and powered by either Pegasus or Perseus engines, the Empire Flying boats were the pride of the British Overseas Airways Corporation, successors of Imperial Airways. Ordered off the drawing board in 1935, the initial order for 28 had been extended by a further 11. These were the "C" class flying boats. In addition, and designed specifically to compete against Pan American's Boeing 314 flying boats, several larger "G" class boats fitted with Hercules engines were intended to operate across the Atlantic ocean.

When the war broke out in September the R.A.F. requisitioned the three "G" class boats along with *"Clio," "Cabot"* and *"Caribou."* These three "C" class aircraft were all destroyed in various actions, the two last-named during the Norwegian Campaign. *"Golden Fleece"* was lost off Cape Finisterre, its crew captured by the Germans. However the services on the Empire network were not initially interrupted because Italy remained neutral. But in 1940 when the German armies swept through the Low Countries and captured Paris Mussolini was emboldened to join his Axis partner. Thereafter the Mediterranean was no longer a safe area over which civilian aircraft could fly,

Two remarkable flights were undertaken by Empire boats as the Germans tank columns raced across France. The first of these, commanded by Captain Anthony Loraine, was to Lake Biscarrosse in the vicinity of Bordeaux. His passengers were emissaries who were hoping to persuade the French government, which had reached that town, to fly with them to Algiers and continue the war. This mission failed and Loraine took off from the lake to return home as German bombers pounded local airfields.

Another flight to Biscarrosse followed shortly afterwards under the command of Captain Donald Bennett. The object was to rescue members of the Polish government who were believed to have reached Bordeaux. By this time France had capitulated and German penetration of the area had been extended. Travelling on board *"Cathay"* was the Polish prime minister General Sikorski. After landing at Biscarrosse the general insisted that he would need until the following morning to gather in his staff. After a very anxious night Bennett was greatly relieved by the reappearance of Sikorski with several carloads of Poles, including his own daughter. Bennett then successfully evaded German reconnaissance aircraft and flew home.

The German occupation of France obliged B.O.A.C. to find a new route to link the British Isles with Africa and the Far East. Loraine was given the task of conducting the proving flight. The chosen destination was Lagos, Nigeria whence a landplane service could link up other British possessions in Africa. The first stage of this new route was to Foynes on the Shannon river in southern Ireland, already equipped to handle the flying boats which had been conducting trials across the North Atlantic Ocean. The next sector was to Lisbon in neutral Portugal and onwards to Bathurst in the Gambia, Freetown in Sierra Leone and finally Lagos.

The longest sector was between Lisbon and Bathurst which took about 14 hours. To carry sufficient fuel and as great a payload as possible the interior of the flying boat was stripped of all furnishings and the floor left bare. No stewards were carried, cold meals in cartons comprising the only fare. Flying *"Clyde"* Loraine successfully solved the problems of moorings and refuelling at the staging posts. On his return to England he would be able to assure B.O.A.C. that the West African route was practicable. However Loraine's journey home was delayed. He received orders to carry French emissaries to Leopoldville in the Belgian Congo, a ten-hour flight away. He landed *"Clyde"* in Stanley Pool which separated Leopoldville from Brazzaville, then under Vichy control. A secret meeting was conducted on *"Clyde"* involving representatives of French Cameroon and Chad. As a result of this the whole of French Equatorial Africa rallied to the Free French banner of General de Gaulle.

A regular service to West Africa was introduced. To provide it B.O.A.C. required some more pilots. In the latter part of 1941 three Boeing flying boats had been purchased from Pan American Airways to operate a service to the United States. The most senior B.O.A.C. captains, among them Kelly Rogers and Loraine, and others holding a navigation licence, had to be replaced. The airline had hoped that the R.A.F. would transfer pilots already trained on flying boats but the ten of us who were posted had flown only landplanes.

The Empire boats were serviced at Hythe, Hampshire, a short distance on the ferry from Southampton, regularly the target of German bombers on night-time raids. We were given a conversion course which included instruction in manoeuvring onto mooring buoys in all conditions of wind and tide. This was rather more difficult than handling the flying boats which were no faster than anything we had flown before. The most important thing to remember was to keep the wings level on touchdown or a wingtip float could be wrenched off. It was also something of a surprise that the Pegasus engines of the "C" class and the Hercules engines of the "G" class did not drive variable-pitch propellers.

Services departed from Poole harbour in daylight with Foynes on the Shannon river in southern Ireland the first stop. The next stage was to Lisbon and was timed to ensure that the aircraft was within the territorial limits of the Iberian peninsula by first light. At Foynes a launch raced ahead of the flying boat, laying flares, whilst the take-off run was conducted swiftly before the wind and tide moved the flares too far out of line. This flight took at least eight hours. With all sound-proofing, furnishing and carpeting removed the aircraft interior was extremely cold and draughty. The primitive heating system rarely worked.

Germany maintained full diplomatic relations with the Irish Republic and Portugal, and German agents kept the Luftwaffe informed of our aircraft movements. Junkers 88s were sometimes observed off the Shannon estuary and regularly patrolled the Western Approaches. Civil airliners were considered legitimate targets and a Douglas DC-3 flying from Lisbon to the British Isles was shot down over the Bay of Biscay. A flying boat carrying two German consular officials who had been interned in England was met on the Tagus by a welcoming party from their embassy. Almost all the passengers on the West African service were involved in the war effort. This included senior military men who necessarily had to travel in civilian clothes.

Cabo Ruivo on the Tagus river, close to the centre of Lisbon, was the flying boat base and was shared with Pan-American Airways. This comprised a jetty and customs shed. It was a startling experience in wartime to find oneself in a brightly-lit city with well-stocked shops and restaurants and with every street-corner kiosk selling both British and German newspapers. The flight crews of Lufthansa and Alitalia used the same hotels as ourselves.

The departure from Lisbon was also made after sunset, the navigation lights being switched off before leaving Portuguese airspace. Weather briefing was provided in the British embassy but this was scanty as allied shipping had ceased to transmit meteorological information that could be useful to the enemy. The window of the weather bureau in the embassy was overlooked by the German embassy next door so was permanently curtained. Even so the arrival and departure of uniformed flight crew was undoubtedly noted and the correct inference drawn.

On the long flight to Bathurst each pilot took turns to handle the flying so it was sometimes possible to sleep on the softer mailbags. Celestial navigation was supplemented by bearings from marine beacons along the African coast, identified by their two-letter code. The French colony of Senegal to the north of Gambia had remained loyal to the puppet Vichy regime so Dakar was given a wide berth, but French aerial activity was negligible. Gambia is subject to rain for eight months of the year, Sierra Leone even longer, but otherwise no severe meteorological problems disrupted the African end of the route. Aircraft which had made the journey from the United States via Natal, in Brazil, used the aerodrome at Bathurst. We turned round in Lagos where our passengers, bound for the North African campaign, were transferred to B.O.A.C. landplanes.

Returning to Britain there was the problem of weather at Lisbon which might have deteriorated during the fourteen-hour flight. Early morning mist and fog is not uncommon. I recall one trip when the captain was sufficiently anxious to request permission to divert to the Canary Islands. The Spanish authorised this but fortunately a signal was received from Lisbon reporting an improvement in the weather. This was just as well as we did not have an adequate chart showing the location of the Spanish flying boat facility. The flight from Lisbon to Foynes was once more conducted in darkness with a dawn landing on the river before flying home to England.

After eighteen months secondment I returned to the R.A.F. During that time *"Clyde"* had been lost in a severe gale lashing the Tagus. *"Clare"* caught fire and crashed off Dakar. *"Golden Horn"* crashed attempting a landing on the Tagus with an engine on fire. These disasters so reduced B.O.A.C.'s fleet at Poole that Short Sunderlands, stripped of their gun turrets, were made available by the R.A.F.

Following Italy's entry into the war Durban in South Africa became the engineering base for services to Cairo and eastward to the Malay States, Australia and New Zealand. The task of the flying boats could scarcely be called routine; several were pressed into service to evacuate British troops from Crete after Germany's successful air invasion. The Japanese attack on Pearl Harbour in December 1941 was followed by their occupation of Thailand, Burma, the Malay States and Dutch East Indies, thereby severing the Empire route to Australia.

Almost unopposed, Japanese Zero fighters ranged the skies over Java and the Timor Sea. Seven of them intercepted *"Corio"* and attacked her. With two engines on fire Captain Koch attempted to put the flying boat down off Koepang, but the sea poured in through the bullet-scarred hull and *"Corio"* sank. Most of the passengers were killed. Koch and one passenger swam ashore and were able to obtain help for the survivors.

On the night of 4th February 1942 the last of the flying boats at Singapore set out for Broome in the Northern Territory of Australia. Ten days later the famous British base fell to the invaders. A shuttle service to supply Dutch and other allied troops in Java was mounted from Broome. This effort was shortlived. At the end of the month *"Circe"* was shot down. Three days later, whilst *"Coriana"* and *"Centaurus"* were at their moorings off Broome, they were attacked and destroyed by enemy fighters.

In March *"Corinthian"* was destroyed at Darwin. *"Calypso"* and *"Camilla"* flew on in support of the Australian forces before both crashed, the former in New Guinea in August and *"Camilla"* in the sea near Port Moresby in April 1943.

Fourteen Empire boats survived the war and were refitted to resume the service. These plied the routes until March 1947 when they were succeeded by several derivatives, the Hythe, Sandringham and Solent. In 1950 B.O.A.C. abandoned flying boat operations. The service was undoubtedly very popular with a leisured class of passenger who travelled in a spacious cabin with nightstops at comfortable resthouses or houseboats on rivers and lakes. It was also hopelessly uneconomic and offered less and less competition to a new generation of pressurised airliners emerging from American factories.

CHAPTER 15

SKY TRAMPS AND SCAMPS IN THE POSTWAR AIR CHARTER SCENE

In 1945 the end of hostilities was followed by the disposal of huge quantities of military aircraft at very low prices. A four-engined bomber could be bought for £100 and spare engines for £5 each. Lacking sufficient airliners the British Overseas Airways Corporation purchased Avro Lancasters and Handley Page Halifaxes and converted them to carry passengers and freight.

An enterprising flight engineer, Freddie Laker, bought a considerable number of machines and acted as a dealer in aircraft and spare parts. His first company, Aviation Traders, did not themselves operate any of these but sold or leased them to others. An early customer was 25-year-old Harold Bamberg. With one partner and a capital of £100 he founded Eagle Aviation and sought contracts to fly passengers and freight. Within a few months 69 independent companies were registered by enthusiasts who had pooled their gratuities and bought one or two war-surplus machines to engage in charter work as sky tramps.

The Labour government which came to power in 1945 gave these entrepreneurs very little encouragement. Its policy was that scheduled services should be the preserve of the airways corporations. British European Airways, the newest of these, swiftly swallowed up those few small domestic airlines which had resumed business. There was to be no poaching of passengers who would otherwise have to buy a ticket on a scheduled service. Moreover the nation's dire financial straits permitted only a minimal amount of foreign currency to be allocated for non-essential foreign travel. Inevitably very many independent companies foundered. An airliner has to be kept in the air ensuring revenue, not on the ground incurring parking fees.

Various international commotions offered the charter companies a lifeline. In 1947, in the wake of their new independent status, the Indian sub-continent erupted with violence as Muslims and Hindus massacred each other. An airlift to rescue refugees provided welcome revenue. The Nizam of Hyderabad, hereditary ruler of that territory, foresaw the threat of invasion by his powerful neighbour. The disturbances gave him time to organise its defence. He required weapons and a British pilot, Sidney Cotton, responded. His company's Lancaster freighters, temporarily based in Pakistan, flew in military supplies. Protests to the British government that India's airspace was being infringed led to the invalidation of Cotton's licence. But the activities of other adventurers suffered no such hindrance. It was an open secret that former R.A.F. pilots had flown aircraft and spares to Palestine soon after it had ceased to be a British protectorate.

The Indian invasion of Hyderabad was overshadowed when the Russians imposed a land and sea blockade on West Berlin. Few expected the resolute response of the Western allies, nor did it seem possible that an airlift of food and fuel could save the Berliners from starvation and the winter weather. Yet the airlift did keep Berlin supplied and 23 British charter companies, some operating only one twin-engined aircraft, backed up the fleets of U.S.A.F. Skymasters and R.A.F. Yorks.

Offered £85 per flying hour, Harold Bamberg put five Halifaxes, each with a freight pannier under the bomb bay, on the run into Berlin. Prices of war surplus aircraft rose but a Halifax could earn a profit of £200 in 24 hours if the weather permitted six trips to be flown.

The largest and most profitable load was the near ten tons of diesel fuel which was carried on the Avro Tudor tankers. Air Vice Marshal Don Bennett's Airflight operated two of these and he personally flew 250 sorties. When the Russians recognised defeat and lifted the blockade a number of charter companies had a healthier bank balance but the competition had become tougher. A war-surplus Douglas Dakota now cost £4,000 but needed to be flown for 20,000 miles each month to earn an adequate return.

The end of the airlift left little scope for operators of Halifaxes. Freddie Laker repurchased many such aircraft, melted them down and sold the metal to manufacturers of saucepans and the like. Harold Bamberg bought three Yorks from B.O.A.C. to carry passengers on charter work. With the return of a Conservative government the private companies suffered less obstruction and obtained trooping contracts. When Laker founded Air Charter Limited to compete for the traffic neglected by the airways corporations Bamberg was to remain his principal rival.

Despite the unexplained loss of two Tudors in the Western Atlantic Don Bennett had never lost confidence in the potential of this aircraft, nor of the intrinsic safety of its design. After the airlift he retitled his company Airflight and engaged in long-distance charter flights.

Another company, William Dempster Limited, then bought two Tudors and offered low-fare flights to South Africa from Stansted. Their chief pilot was Polish-born Marion Kozubski whose war service had been rewarded by the Polish Cross of Valeur. Subsequently he had taken part in the Indian and Berlin airlifts. William Dempster Limited encountered legal difficulties when they were charged with selling tickets to passengers who were not members of the party on whose behalf the charter was undertaken. In 1953 the company ceased trading.

Laker had also recognised the good economics of the Tudor. He bought as many as he could find, adopted the modifications recommended by the Air Registration Board and installed a huge freight door. By purchasing Bennett's company he acquired a profitable German air-freight contract and added to that a British government contract to carry stores to the rocket range in Woomera. The Tudor was renamed the Supertrader and far exceeded the performance of the version rejected by B.O.A.C. in 1947.

Marion Kozubski believed that he had learned enough to run his own airline. He and other airline pilots pooled their resources to found Independent Air Transport. Acting as both chairman and managing director he started operations with one Avro Anson which was later replaced by two de Havilland Doves. Among their tasks were flights to ferry racing pigeons to their starting point in France. By July 1957 Kozubski was operating nine Vickers Vikings and had taken possession of a Douglas DC-4. The maintenance base was at Hurn. Charters were flown from Heathrow, Blackbushe and Manchester.

The general public first became aware of Kozubski through a bizarre incident on New Year's Eve 1957. Flying the DC-4 from Dusseldorf to Damascus he encountered bad weather and flew over Albania to avoid it. MiG fighters were sent up to intercept him and he was forced to land at Valona. Several days passed before crew and passengers were permitted to resume their flight.

In the hostile economic climate which had witnessed the demise of so many small companies Kozubski acted as a slave-driver to stay in business. In May 1958 Independent Air Transport was the first company to be convicted, on ten charges, for breaches of regulations covering flight-time regulations. This prosecution did not produce any serious change in policy. Moreover it was the practice of the company to send on a flight an engineer, who was not licensed, to certify any work of maintenance or rectification to the aircraft. At Hurn maintenance work was carried out by tired men working a 60-hour week under pressure and without instruction or supervision.

That September an overloaded Viking freighter left Heathrow en route to Israel. An engine gave trouble and the captain turned back to land at Blackbushe. Unable to maintain a safe altitude the aircraft crashed in Southall killing all the occupants. The resulting enquiry revealed that the crew had had insufficient rest before take-off; that two men who had endeavoured unsuccessfully to remedy an engine fault before take-off were not trained engineers; that the aircraft was deliberately overloaded by omitting from the load sheet the weight of the stands and blocks upon which two Proteus engines were stowed. It was obvious to the court that this had been done to avoid documenting the overload, which would have made necessary a landing at Lyons, in addition to Nice, en route to Israel.

In the words of Mr Justice Phillimore who presided over the enquiry: "Personnel were largely recruited from the airways corp-orations or larger companies who had lost that employment or would scarcely have been elegible for employment with a company of established reputation."

Such men were susceptible to pressure to evade regulations designed to ensure safety of operation. The enquiry also estab-lished that the company had failed to comply with the regulations about pilots' competency checks. The Viking's co-pilot had less than 1,000 hours total flying and only about 24 hours on twin-engined aircraft. The court accepted that Captain William Bright, the chief pilot, had repeatedly pressed for proper facilities to check the competency of pilots. Kozubski had steadfastly refused.

To quote the assessors again: "The attitude of the company was remarkable. Those directors who gave evidence put the whole blame for the accident upon the captain . . . they were not prepared to admit any criticism of their own action or that the action of the captain might have been affected by the policy of the company . . . that policy was to keep its aircraft in the air and gainfullly employed regardless of the regulations . . . the short fact is that it was being run in a manner designed to keep expense to the minimum and that proper training and checking facilities were deliberately refused with this object in view."

In the course of the enquiry the court had heard the evidence of 55 witnesses. Captain Kozubski had not been one of them. On the first day of the enquiry he sold out his majority shareholding and was very shortly to register another company. The new management of Independent Air Transport took great pains to remedy the practices of their predecessors. The bad publicity which had been attracted led them to adopt a new title, Blue Air. The former chief pilot, William Bright, was retained in his post. Their fortunes however did not recover and by the end of 1959 the company collapsed, putting 120 employees out of work.

Captain Bright was an experienced pilot who had flown for both B.O.A.C. and Eagle Aviation. After Blue Air's collapse he worked for another company whose directors he had to sue to obtain the salary due to him. Then he turned to freelance work and hired a Viking to look for loads in the Congo, arriving as the grant of national independence was accompanied by insurrections. After that it might have seemed mere routine to be engaged to ferry to England a Douglas DC-4 sold to his employer by Capitol Airways in Washington.

In airline service the normal crew of a DC-4 was two pilots. a navigator and a radio operator. To save money Bright's employer told him to manage with just one other pilot who would join him in Washington. This man never showed up. Undaunted, Bright flew the machine single-handed from Washington to London airport, determined to claim the fee which would have been due to the missing co-pilot.

Next Bright registered World Wide Aviation with £3,000 and a partner who put up £1,000. He leased a DC-4 and, in addition to revenue from seasonal charters, he obtained a contract to operate a transatlantic service for the Icelandic airline. Bright hired a second DC-4 and was engaged by the Belgian Airline Sabena to support United Nations operations in the Congo. The failure of another company whose passengers were stranded abroad encouraged Bright to lease a third DC-4; but World Wide Aviation was grossly undercapitalised and in a year that saw the collapse of ten other companies Bright was grounded once more.

In the same month that Kozubski sold Independent Air Transport he founded Falcon Airways and bought a Viking to undertake a series of inclusive-tour holiday flights from Black-bushe. The following year three Handley Page Hermes were acquired and sometimes operated charters to North America. By 1960 when a DC-4 was leased Falcon Airways had earned a good reputation for efficiency and reliability. In 1961 the existing fleet was replaced by four Lockheed Constellations.

A charter to carry emigrants from Guyana was obtained. A government inspector who examined the Constellation chosen for the task recommended that it be fitted with a roof-mounted periscopic sextant and Loran navigation equipment. The company failed to install the former and the aircraft departed for Guyana under Kozubski's command with the Loran fitted but not checked for serviceability. On the return journey 68 emigrants were boarded and landings made at Stephenville and Gander. The Loran was definitely unserviceable. In addition a baby on board was found to be suffering from pneumonia.

Kozubski decided upon a route to reach Gatwick in the shortest possible time. This route passed beyond the range of any land which lay within 90 minutes flying time. This would have been legal if sufficient life-rafts had been carried in the Constellation to accommodate all on board. The number of life-rafts available was well short of that figure. As a consequence of these events Falcon

Airways and Kozubski were charged with seven counts of breach of regulations. The airline lost the case and incurred fines and costs.

Thereafter the Air Registration Board took a particular interest in the condition of all three Constellations. Two spent much of the summer on the ground awaiting conversion. The Air Transport Licensing Board was not sympathetic to Falcon's application to operate inclusive-tour flights to Malaya and Tangier. The company had intended to operate four Constellations but it was frustrated by a series of problems. In September 1961 their Air Operator's Certificate was withdrawn. Shortly afterwards Falcon Airways was placed in the hands of a receiver.

This was not the last company with which Kozubski was associated. He was a pilot with Ace Freighters, flying DC-4s and Constellations. Within two years this company too was put into liquidation.

Despite battles over route licences Harold Bamberg was still in business twenty years after the founding of Eagle Aviation. He had acquired Boeing 707s and planned to operate scheduled services to New York, Bermuda and the Caribbean. Then his bankers, fearful of the losses the airline would incur in the approaching winter season, withdrew their support: the end had come.

Freddie Laker's airline lasted rather longer but suffered the same fate. He had bought Douglas DC-10s in the expectation that the American government would allow him to operate a no-reservation service to New York. The British government had designated Laker Airways as an Atlantic carrier. While waiting for U.S. approval Laker's plans were frustrated when the home government reversed their decision to allow him to compete against British Airways on this route.

His fortunes improved with the return of a Conservative government. His low fare "Skytrain" service to New York was extremely popular, enticing a new class of world traveller into the air. Laker became a popular hero and was awarded a knighthood. The principal carriers on the North Atlantic were not slow to retaliate by reducing their own fares. The fall in sterling against the dollar greatly increased the burden of interest incurred by Laker in his purchase of American aircraft. Sir Freddie had no more success than Harold Bamberg in rallying further financial support and his airline ceased trading.

British Eagle and Laker Airways were but two of the sky tramp companies which had grown and struggled to compete against more powerful airlines supported and protected by governments against independent predators. Many smaller companies have suffered the same fate but applications for licences to operate services do not cease.

A former airline director summed it up: "A man with lots of flying experience finds a man with money and they start an airline. After a time the former has more flying experience but the latter has lost his money."

CHAPTER 16

SELLING THE SUPER VC.10

The pilots loved it. The passengers welcomed the quiet cabin. At the worst possible moment B.O.A.C.'s new chairman tried to cancel the entire order.

The VC.10 owed its origins to the specification for a long-range transport aircraft intended for the R.A.F. Codenamed V.1000 it was to be shaped like the Vickers Valiant with four Rolls Royce Conways fitted in the wing root. The initial order was for six aircraft but in 1955, a few months before the first flight, the Transport Aircraft Requirements Committee cancelled it.

Shortly after this the British Overseas Airways Corporation was faced with the need to order a jet airliner to compete on the North Atlantic route. The Boeing 707 had been ordered in large numbers by the United States Air Force and their development of it was sparing potential airline customers the great burden of that initial expense. Consequently B.O.A.C. asked the British government, which controlled the purse strings, to be allowed to order 17 Boeing 707s, to be powered by Rolls Royce Conway engines.

At the same time B.O.A.C. had a requirement for an airliner which could carry an adequate payload from aerodromes situated at a high altitude in a tropical climate. Typical of these were Johannesburg, Nairobi and Harare (Salisbury). Among British aircraft constructors only Vickers offered a design sufficiently close to B.O.A.C.'s performance specifications. Moreover Vickers did not intend to ask the government for financial support. With the advantage of their original work on the V.1000 they envisaged an airliner with four engines mounted below a massive T-shaped tailplane. This design was also favoured by aerodynamicists at the R.A.E., Farnborough. Even before discussions began with B.O.A.C. such was the shape of the airliner that Vickers proposed to build.

The Minister for Civil Aviation was Harold Watkinson. Sir Miles Thomas had just retired as chairman of B.O.A.C. In his own words: "I was tired of irksome political interference . . . you can either have an airline run as a competitive keen commercial concern using the best equipment or you can have it as a shop window for British aircraft that you would not normally purchase."

His successor was a director of British European Airways, Sir Gerard d'Erlanger, who acted as part-time chairman with only two full-time directors on the board. One of these, Basil Smallpeice, the managing director, was continuously a member of the board until the end of 1963.

Watkinson was prepared to allow B.O.A.C. to order 15 Boeings for the North Atlantic route, but it was made clear to d'Erlanger and Smallpeice that the government could stop any subsequent order going abroad by withholding the necessary dollars. Some years later, giving evidence to a Select Committee, Smallpeice said that when the VC.10 order was being considered: "We had been told quite flatly that if we did not order a British aircraft we would not get any . . . it was a question of the VC.10 or nothing."

In 1956 the Vickers machine was not intended for the North Atlantic route. This role came to be considered later when it was realised that the aircraft's superb handling qualities and quiet cabin would compensate for any deficiency in economy of operation by proving attractive selling points. B.O.A.C. was often accused of being pro-American, and there were good historical reasons for this. As a result of the rearmament programme begun in 1935 the production of civil aircraft was accorded a very low priority. Consequently the airline's ageing landplane fleet had before the war been described as "the laughing stock of Europe." When hostilities began a North Atlantic passenger service had only been made possible by the purchase of three Boeing flying boats.

After the war B.O.A.C. had bought Lockheed Constellations and Boeing Stratocruisers. When the delivery of the turboprop Bristol Britannias was seriously delayed Douglas DC-7s were acquired to fill the gap. The pure-jet Comet 4 was smaller than the Boeing 707 and could not fly non-stop to New York. There was every likelihood that later versions of the American airliner would be able to do so.

B.O.A.C. decided to take a maximum of 25 VC.10s but Vickers would not accept any order lower than 35 and did not expect to break even until 45 were sold. The problem in the British aircraft manufacturing industry was that any order was invariably too small for the manufacturer or too big for B.O.A.C., the only domestic airline likely to require more than a modest number of airliners. The board felt obliged to agree to the figure of 45 and by January 1958 had signed a contract for 35 aircraft with options on the others to be exercised by 1962. During 1958 and 1959 Vickers offered a stretched version of the VC.10 which came to be called the Super VC.10. Following arguments over prices the contract was rewritten in June 1960 for ten Super VC.10s to be delivered, following the completion of the order for standard VC.10s, and the last of seven more in 1969.

When the possibility of operating the British aircraft on the North Atlantic was considered by the board of B.O.A.C. their technical staff were not in favour. Doubts were expressed about the likelihood of obtaining delivery and certification within a reasonable timescale. For B.O.A.C. the "optimum economic design" would have been an aircraft with four engines in pods under the wing. This proposal, according to d'Erlanger's successor, Sir Matthew Slattery, "was ruled out on political grounds," and maybe on Vickers' commercial grounds as well. Britain would not copy an American aircraft. B.O.A.C.'s technical experts remained unhappy about the proposals, particularly as Vickers were not willing to guarantee the performances that the R.A.E. believed could be achieved.

1959 had been a bad year for B.O.A.C. Trading conditions were difficult. The changeover of fleets had been costly and interest on capital increased. The accounts showed a deficit. D'Erlanger complained that the corporation incurred far higher expense in introducing British aircraft such as the Comet 4 and Britannia than if it had ordered an American airliner because the development costs were incurred by the first operator.

The following year Sir Matthew Slattery replaced d'Erlanger as chairman. Before assuming office he asked the latter not to commit B.O.A.C. to the additional ten VC.10s.

He was told: "I am sorry. It is too late. I have been under very strong pressure from the minister (Duncan Sandys) to do this."

He had been warned by Sir George Edwards, chairman of Vickers, that production of the VC.10 would not go ahead without the additional order. Remembering B.O.A.C.'s desperate shortage of aircraft when the original Comet 1 was grounded he did not want to be put in that position again.

D'Erlanger added: "I never believed that it was the corporation's job to make profits. The corporation was there to support the British aircraft industry, to develop the routes around the world. My difficulty was to do that without letting the staff of B.O.A.C. feel that money did not matter, that they did not have to be businesslike."

During 1961 B.O.A.C. had second thoughts about the size of the Super VC.10 and asked Vickers to reduce its length. In December, following Treasury concern over capital expenditure the types and numbers of VC.10s were settled at 12 Standards and 20 Supers. Unfortunately the expected rise in traffic had not materialised. Revenue fell off during the financial year 1961/62 whilst the increased capacity offered was 32% greater than during the previous year. Losses were high, made worse by interest on capital, the losses of B.O.A.C.'s associated companies and obsolescence provisions on propeller aircraft.

The prototype VC.10 made its first flight in May 1962 at about the time Julian Amery was appointed Minister of Aviation. In a memo to the new minister Slattery warned him that it would not be realistic for the corporation to be purely commercial in its outlook.

"To expect a company to do something that is not wholly commercial and then, when it has lost money doing it, to expect it to pay interest on that money is bloody crazy."

He asked the government to write off the huge accumulated deficit and to provide a subsidy for developing the VC.10. The House of Commons heard Amery reject this advice in terms of contempt.

In July the minister appointed Mr John Corbett to investigate B.O.A.C.'s position and prospects. In the spring of 1963 the corporation's trading situation was such that Smallpeice declared that "the foreseeable workload ahead of us in four years time is less than it was by ten large aircraft." He calculated that a 13% annual growth in passenger miles and a quadrupling of freight ton-miles would be needed by 1968 to fill all the VC.10s on order. Vickers were asked to suspend work on ten VC.10s.

When Amery received Corbett's report he chose not to disclose its contents, either to the Board of B.O.A.C. or to the House of Commons

In November a government White Paper was published containing criticisms of the airline's financial handling. In a BBC interview Amery accused Slattery and Smallpeice of "very serious weakness in management." He obtained the resignations of both men and invited Sir Giles Guthrie, a banker, to take over as chairman on January 1st 1964. Guthrie was allowed to read only parts of the Corbett report.

The new chairman must have known that B.O.A.C.'s financial problems could not be attributed entirely to his predecessors. Arm-twisting over aircraft procurement, late delivery of aircraft and the drain of money to support numerous associated companies had all contributed. Guthrie asked Amery for an assurance that B.O.A.C. would be compensated if directed to order a particular airliner against its commercial judgement.

"The choice of aircraft," Amery wrote back, "is a matter for the corporation's judgement. It has been the aim of the corporation to buy aircraft, as far as possible, from British sources and I trust that this policy will continue . . . If the national interest should appear, either to the corporation or to the government, to acquire some departure from the strict commercial decisions of the corporation this should only be done with the express agreement or at the express request of the minister."

Meanwhile flight crews were undergoing instruction on the VC.10 prior to its introduction on the routes. The pilots were delighted with the aircraft's performance and handling qualities. The quietness of the passenger cabin as a consequence of the rear-mounted engines ensured an equally favourable reaction from the travelling public. The VC.10 was one of the few aircraft to be certified to 60,000 flying hours without a major structural rework. Sir George Edwards, chairman of Vickers, acknowledging that the aircraft was going to enter service several years after the first American jets, pointed out that it offered significant improvements, such as the ability to carry a substantial payload over long distances from 'difficult' aerodromes. At that time a Boeing 707 or

Douglas DC-8 could not have lifted any sort of payload from an airport like Nairobi non-stop to London.

In May 1964 the VC.10 entered service on African routes, but rumours were already rife that Guthrie was pressing the minister to be allowed to cancel a significant number of the Super VC.10s and to be permitted to buy more Boeing 707s. Denigrators of the British aircraft claimed that it would need to carry eight extra passengers on each flight to cover the excess cost. British newspapers, which had been reporting the favourable reception of the aircraft by the travelling public, expressed shock and surprise at the latest turn of events.

B.O.A.C.'s chief engineer, Charles Abell, revealed his misgivings. The Super VC.10, due to enter service on the North Atlantic, had a volumetric capacity and passenger-seat capacity less than the Boeing 707. The gross weight and empty weight of the British aircraft was significantly higher. Obviously it would cost more to operate it. To the claim that it was designed by Vickers to meet a requirement outlined by B.O.A.C. for its eastern and southern routes he pointed out that B.O.A.C. did not design it, nor specify the shape of the wing, nor where the engines should be placed. It had not specified that it should be less economic than its competitors.

By an ironic twist of fate B.O.A.C.'s revenue was rising sharply. The accounts for 1963/64 revealed the highest-ever operating surplus and a million passengers had been carried. Guthrie acknowledged that the credit for this turnaround was due to his predecessors on the Board. Load factors on the VC.10 were running at 90% on some routes, 80% on West African services. The load factor on Central and South African flights had reached 98%. Meanwhile Guthrie had stunned the minister by putting forward his plan to cancel all the Super VC.10s and to buy 14 more Boeing 707s. These, he decided, would be considerably more economic to operate and B.O.A.C. would also benefit from access to the spares pool available to Boeing operators worldwide.

In July 1964 the House of Commons debated the report of a Select Committee into the affairs of B.O.A.C. A remarkable statement by the minister, Julian Amery, contained the following words:

"No advice or instruction was given to B.O.A.C. with regard to the VC.10 order . . . what I have always said is that the chairman of B.O.A.C. should give us his judgement on commercial solutions and he should not seek to determine what the national interest is . . . many of the troubles of the corporation have arisen because the chairman sometimes thought he was judging where the national interest lay."

Given the recent history of B.O.A.C. at the time that Guthrie was appointed as chairman Amery ought to have foreseen the sort of report that he would receive. He might have expected that his terms of reference would be seen by Guthrie as an open invitation to reverse the order for Super VC.10s. But having received this request Amery rejected it; he told the House of Commons that B.O.A.C. had been directed to accept 17 of the Super VC.10s with a futher 10 in abeyance and that three would be diverted to the R.A.F.

The reaction from many members of both main parties was scathing.

For the opposition Roy Jenkins declared that "the terms of reference represented a certain recipe for doing great damage to the 'plane at one of the most vulnerable points in its history."

Another member recalled that after his appointment as chairman Guthrie had been photographed in front of a VC.10, saying: "This is surely a magnificent aircraft."

A full page advertisement in *"The Times"* claimed that the aircraft put B.O.A.C. six years ahead of any other airline in the world."

An air correspondent wrote that Guthrie "did not merely wield an axe. He set about poleaxing the entire Super VC.10 project."

Few would disagree with the remark by Sir Arthur Harvey in the Commons that "they had debated one of the worst messes seen in the House for many years."

Within a year of the VC.10's entry into service B.O.A.C. applied to the Air Registration Board for an increase in the permitted period between overhauls from 4,000 to 6,000 hours. Established rivals only reached this after six years in operation. The Super VC.10 entered service across the North Atlantic in April 1965. During the next three months its average load factor was 74.9%. In

September when the load factor for VC.10s on all routes was 76.1% the load factor for the Super VC.10 was 84.6%.

The airliner was certified for automatic landings years before its American rivals. With an engine out of service a take-off on the other three presented no further problems. The VC.10 was equipped to carry a spare engine in a pod under the wing. The pilots loved the aircraft and got accustomed to a question frequently asked by passengers: "What is so wrong with the VC.10 that your chairman did not want to accept it?" Sadly the damage to any prospect of future sales had been done.

Eventually B.O.A.C. received only 17 Super VC.10s. East African Airways bought five, British United Airways purchased three and Ghana Airways just two. The R.A.F. received fourteen.

Whilst Boeing continued to develop and improve a series of re-engined 707s no such treatment was accorded to the VC.10. But B.O.A.C. operated profitably during each successive year after 1964 and continued using the VC.10 fleet until the end of March 1982. The R.A.F. then acquired these together with spare parts.

Their VC.10s played a valuable part in both the Falklands and Gulf wars and still remain in service in 1998.

In 1964 after completing B.O.A.C.'s conversion course I had moved to a village adjoining Brize Norton. Shortly afterwards the R.A.F.'s own VC.10 squadron was formed there and I was invited to become an honorary member of the Officers' Mess. As it happened I had been stationed at Brize in 1942.

In April 1998 I was invited to the station once again to meet the Air Officer Commanding and was shown over two VC.10s which I had flown twenty years earlier in British Airways; one of these had been converted for in-flight refuelling. I was not at all surprised to be told of the high regard accorded by the squadron pilots to their veteran machines.

PART 3

"HOSTAGES TO FATE"

CHAPTER 17

AIRSHIP R.101:

THE HUMAN FACTOR IN THE DISASTER

Early this century the Germans led the world in airship design and during the first World War their Zeppelins made air raids over England. These were the rigid type about which very little was known in this country. When several were shot down more or less intact they were closely examined. Thereafter the British built a small number of rigid airships on very similar lines, the designers adopting the identical size of the German girders.

The most successful copy of the German Zeppelin was the R.34, which in July 1919 made a return journey between England and New York. It was commanded by Major G.H. Scott and on board was Air Commodore Maitland, the senior officer of the British Airship Service. The flight time to New York was 108 hours and the return journey time was 75 hours. This achievement brought to Scott fame and great respect. It also focussed attention on the commercial potential of airships in the new era of peace.

Several small airlines were already competing against each other to carry passengers and mail to Europe. Up to ten passengers could be flown in converted military aeroplanes but little further than Paris in any one stage. The cruising speed then achieved was not much faster than that of an airship. Some of those whose aim was a commercial air transport service linking Great Britain with the Empire were convinced that for many years to come the airship would offer great advantages in range and load capacity over the aeroplane.

Under construction was an even larger airship, the R.38, which was intended as an advance on the Zeppelin. The detail design was largely the work of the draughtsmen of Short Brothers who stayed on at the Royal Airship Works at Cardington until the R.38 was ready for air tests in 1921. The first few tests had proved so satisfactory that the captain decided to carry out turns at full helm and at full speed. In August, on a perfect day, R.38 was over the Humber on its fourth test. Among those on board was Air Commodore Maitland. The manoeuvres performed caused the airship to break up and catch fire, with the loss of 44 lives.

The enquiry revealed that the constructors had made no calculations whatsoever on the aerodynamic forces to which R.38 would be subjected in such a test.

At that time one of those in the aeroplane construction industry was Nevil Shute Norway. He was working for de Havilland at Stag Lane. Today he is best remembered as a very successful novelist but he was to play an important role in the airship story. He was astonished and greatly shocked by the contents of the accident report, particularly the fact that nobody at Cardington lost their job, nor was even censured after the findings were published.

The government had already reached the view that future airship construction should be left to those private commercial interests prepared to fund it. However, an Imperial conference held in London that summer discussed, among other matters, the possibility of an airship service to major cities of the Empire. Serving on an Air Ministry advisory panel was Commander Dennistown Burney, an ardent advocate for airships. In March 1922 he proposed that Vickers and Shell should take over all the remaining British airship assets; Vickers should build six airships with development costs largely falling upon the public purse. A year later the Conservative government accepted in principle these proposals.

Then the resignation of Stanley Baldwin was followed by the entry into office of the first Labour government, led by Ramsay MacDonald. The latter's choice as Secretary of State for Air was Christopher Thomson, a product of the Royal Military Academy, Woolwich and the Staff College, an intellectual who had attracted attention as the youngest major in the army, before resigning as a Brigadier in 1919. He had contested unsuccessfully two elections in the Labour interest but had been held in such high regard by the outgoing administration that he had been appointed to the Air Ministry advisory panel. On this panel were two senior air officers, Sir Geoffrey Salmond and Sir William Sefton Brancker. Elevated to the House of Lords Thomson revealed his commitment to airship development by taking the title "of Cardington."

Inevitably, Burney's proposal that the government should meet most of the costs and assume all the financial risks of airship development offended the Labour party's principles. After prolonged discussion it was decided to authorise the construction of two airships, each of a certain size, speed and load capacity. The Air Ministry would build one at the Royal Airship Works at Cardington: this became known as R.101. Vickers would construct the other one to the same specification. A subsidiary of Vickers, the Airship Guarantee Company, was given the fixed contract to build R.100 at Howden, Yorkshire, a wartime airship station.

The original specification required each airship to have a capacity of five million cubic feet (hydrogen). The accommodation for 100 passengers should include provision for sleeping, eating and sanitary facilities. Fuel capacity should be for 57 hours flying. The airships should be capable of averaging 63 mph over 48 hours with a top speed of not less than 70 mph. The final trial should involve a satisfactory flight to India with an intermediate stop in Egypt for refuelling under tropical conditions.

R.100 was to follow established practice as an essentially commercial craft; her engines would run on petrol. R.101 was intended to advance the state of the art with innovations in structure, engines, gasbag wiring and valves. The engines should run on diesel fuel. Current thinking extolled the economy of diesel fuel together with its increased safety factor. Diesel engines gave off no inflammable vapour in tropical conditions. This view led to a change of plan over the long distance trial for R.100: Canada was substituted for India. Both airships would be inflated with hydrogen.

Within a year the Labour government lost office but their successors adopted the agreed programme, which envisaged the first flights of each airship in 1927. Sir Samuel Hoare replaced Lord Thomson. The Chief Designer of the R.100 was Barnes Wallis who had been involved in airship design since 1913 and was also Vickers' Chief Engineer. The Managing Director was Burney. Among their team and ultimately to be Chief Calculator and Deputy Chief Engineer was Nevil Shute Norway. He considered

Wallis to be the greatest engineer in the country at that time. Of Burney he wrote: " . . . the keenest engineering imagination of anyone I ever met, coupled with a great commercial sense." Unfortunately Burney and Wallis possessed quite different temperaments and had difficulty working together.

The Chief Designer of R.101 was Colonel Vincent Richmond. He worked alongside the Director of Airship Development at Cardington, Wing Commander Reginald Colmore, who had been involved with airships from their start. Regrettably the hope of both Thomson and Hoare that the two design teams would cooperate amicably was frustrated by Wallis who rebuffed the overtures of Richmond. As time went by R.100's team grew increasingly irritated by the very favourable publicity accorded by the newspapers to R.101 to the exclusion of any great interest in developments at Howden. In addition they were very conscious that the fixed-price contract put them under severe financial constraints, reducing desirable expenditure on research. It was their belief that their rivals had the advantage of generous financial support from the government.

The Germans were building a commercial airship, the *"Graf Zeppelin,"* and it had been hoped that both the British contenders would be completed before she was ready. But thanks to their far greater experience of rigid airships *"Graf Zeppelin"* made her first flight in 1927 and had been flown to Brazil and back in 1928. The two British airships were not flown until the autumn of 1929. There were many reasons for the delay, not least the various government departments claiming the right to influence decisions: the Air Ministry, the Royal Airship Works, the Aeronautical Inspection Directorate and the Department of Civil Aviation.

On her 60th flight *"Graf Zeppelin,"* commanded by the veteran airship commander Dr Eckener, was flown to Cardington and those present were astonished at the superb handling by her crew, all attired in a smart uniform. The airship was moored within fifteen minutes of coming into sight and departed half an hour later carrying Brancker and Richmond on a visit to the German base at Friedrichstrafen.

When the Labour party won the 1929 general election Lord Thomson returned to his former post as Air Minister. It was not the fault of his predecessor, Sir Samuel Hoare, that the programme had slipped back several years. The latter was an aviation enthusiast who delighted in using aircraft on official business and had flown to India. But he had received no encouragement from Stanley Baldwin, who regarded flying as inherently dangerous. The London *"Morning Post"* had criticised Hoare, reminding him that his office was in Whitehall and that he should only use "the established forms of transport."

In 1925 the airship shed at Cardington had been enlarged, a new high mast erected, contracts placed for the construction of airship bases in Cairo and Karachi. It had been the intention that two old airships, R.33 and R.36, should be refurbished and flown to Cairo to gather data but this did not happen. R.33, built in 1917, had to be taken out of service due to severe corrosion. The government was unwilling to meet the expense of reconditioning R.36.

R.101 suffered from the programme of ambitious unproven technological innovations which it had been hoped to incorporate: these caused delays. The diesel engines not only gave 20% less power than expected but were far too heavy. Richmond's request to substitute petrol engines was rejected. The fate of the men on R.38 who had died in the pools of burning fuel in the Humber remained a vivid memory. He was reminded that diesel fuel was cheaper and the rate of consumption was so much lower that there was a considerable compensation for the weight penalty. Nevertheless it was obvious that R.101 could not meet her design targets so a series of measures to lighten her were introduced. The passenger accommodation was greatly reduced and an extra bay was incorporated to increase gas capacity by another half a million cubic feet.

In October 1929 R.101 made her first flight, followed a few weeks later by R.100. The officers allocated to the airships were headed by Major Scott who had made the return flight to the United States in 1919. He was the holder of Airship Licence No. 1. Squadron Leader Booth was designated to command R.100 with Captain G. Meager as Chief Navigator. Flight Lieutenant C. Irwin was given command of R.101 with Squadron Leader Johnston as Chief Navigator.

Each airship conducted trial flights around the British Isles during the following six months and a number of technical problems were encountered. R.100's second-hand engines gave trouble and had to be replaced by six Rolls Royce Condors. The Chief Designer of R.101 was concerned about the weight and performance of the diesel engines. With its power car each weighed over three tons. One was used only for going astern near the mooring mast. Ultimately five Beardmore Tornado diesel engines were fitted. Both airships suffered from gas leaks caused by chafing of the bags against the girders. An attempt to cure this by padding brought a threat from the Inspector in charge of Airworthiness to deny an extension of the "permit to fly" unless a better solution was found.

A compromise was reached. Tears in the fabric of the airship's outer covers often occurred. The covers were under the greatest stress at the upper range of speed. By reducing speed temporary repairs could be made in flight. Sheets of cotton fabric were carried on board for such an eventuality, together with dope.

In the course of the flight trials of R.100 her commander, Ralph Booth, reported that the speed achieved was greater than the specification required but that the lift was less. He complained about gasbag leaks and was most concerned about the airship's outer covers which he wanted replaced. They were three years old and had been stored in far from ideal conditions. Neither the Air Ministry nor the contractors were prepared to incur the expense. Masses of dope were put on the top half of the covers and in heavy rain a cascade of water would fall between the bags.

The outer covers of R.101 were equally suspect. In his book *"Slide Rule"* N.S. Norway, best known to the public as the author Nevil Shute, revealed that the Cardington engineers were so concerned about their problems that they had suggested to Burney that both airship staffs should jointly ask for a postponement of the Canada and India flights. Burney rejected this, insisting that R.100 was ready and capable of flying to Canada. At the time the world was engulfed in a major economic crisis following the Wall Street crash. The Airship Guarantee Company was losing money on its fixed contract. Burney had already been obliged to lay off nearly all his men. It was understood that if any more airships were to be ordered either Cardington or Howden would get the contract, not both. The two groups of employees were desperate to set in train their final long-distance trials.

When R.100 set off for Canada on 29th July she had completed seven trial flights and her outer covers had stood up to the stress of three hours continuous flying at 70 mph. Captain Scott was on board but he was under orders to restrict his function to advice to the airship captain, R. Booth, who could choose not to accept it. Nor could Scott give orders to any of the crew. He lacked recent airship flying experience and was held in very much less respect than in previous years by those who had to work with him. Burney travelled on the flight, as did Norway. There were several other passengers and 37 crew.

The trip to Canada was conducted in fair weather without any serious problems. About 125 miles from the city of Quebec all six engines were opened up in an attempt to reach Montreal before dusk. The air became more turbulent and for about a minute this was very severe. An inspection revealed rents up to three feet long in various parts of the outer cover. Speed was reduced to allow repairs to be made.

Halfway between Quebec and Montreal a line squall was observed ahead across the airship's path, dark clouds with heavy rain beneath. There was ample fuel remaining and it would have caused little delay to fly around the squall. Scott, however, ordered the helmsman to hold his course. Booth was present and it may be that at this late stage of the flight he was disinclined to countermand Scott's instruction and to assert his own authority. Swiftly the airship was engulfed in heavy rain and caught in a strong upcurrent. From the normal cruising level of 1,500 feet R.100 was carried up to 4,500 feet and at one point the nose was down at an angle of 35 degrees. A drum of red dope, a highly inflammable liquid, toppled over and poured its contents into the control car. This was the worst storm the airship had experienced. Flight continued with all lights extinguished to avoid a spark igniting the dope.

At dawn R.100 moored at St. Hubert airport near Montreal, having flown 3,300 statute miles. Within a few days all the defects had been repaired. After some local flights to demonstrate the airship to the Canadians the homeward journey was completed in 57 hours. This was the last flight to be made by R.100.

Everyone at Cardington now felt themselves under great pressure to have R.101 in proper shape for the required flight to India. Lord Thomson had been prevented from travelling to Canada by his Cabinet duties but he had compelling reasons to journey on R.101 to India. The departure date was delayed a few times before being set for early in October. There was an Imperial Conference being held in London at that time and it was Thomson's ambition to return from a successful flight to India to be appointed as the new Viceroy. For this flight Major Scott would once again be nominally in charge with Flight Lieutenant Irwin in actual command of the airship. The second in command was Lieutenant Commander Atherstone. The latter voiced complaints that there had been a lack of consultation between Scott and the flying staff under his control. Scott sometimes instructed the crew to take over the airship for a flight with the minimum of notice.

Irwin had demanded: "a night of 24 hours duration under reasonably adverse conditions, to be followed by a night of 48 hours under adverse conditions; the ship to have flown at least six hours continuously at full speed through bumpy conditions and the rest of the flight at cruising speed. After landing a complete bow-to-stern examination to be carried out."

Late in September the Chief Inspector made his final survey before R.101 was signed out to leave Cardington. He observed that there had been serious deterioration of the fabric of the outer cover. Colmore and Richmond were informed that "a finger could be pushed through the cover." The former ordered reinforcing strips to be stuck down with red dope over the affected areas.

A schedule for the imminent flight to India had been issued by the Air Ministry to all R.A.F. stations along the route to India. R.101 had done most of its test flying on three of its five engines at 50 knots. The loads on the outer cover would have been almost doubled at 63 knots. If a split had developed in daylight or in good weather this would have been serious: if this should happen at night in rough air the consequences were incalculable. Time was running out. When the final test was carried out on 1st October the air cooler of one engine failed. The weather was fine and conditions very calm. The full-speed trial had to be abandoned.

R.101 had not flown for even an hour at full speed at any time nor in any really adverse conditions. There had been a recent appointment of a new Air Member for Supply and research, Air Vice Marshal Hugh Dowding. But he had never been in an airship in his life and felt obliged to accept any advice offered to him from Cardington. He was told that both the *"Graf Zeppelin"* and R.100 had set out on their first overseas nights after fewer trials than R.101. The airship had been flown for a total of 103 hours and all the known defects had been corrected.

Lord Thomson had stated more than once, in Parliament and in public, that the safety of the airship was of supreme importance. Yet, in July, he had minuted: "I must insist on the programme for the Indian flight being adhered to as I have made my plans accordingly."

The schedule had already slipped three years. Richmond and Colmore were tired and harassed men who had done their best within their own knowledge of airship technology and in the time scale permitted to them. They must have felt under great pressure to follow upon R.100's successful flight. They agreed that R.101 would be ready to set off for India on the evening of 4th October.

One last formality remained. A Certificate of Airworthiness was a legal document for flights over foreign territory. The members of the Air Council and the Air Ministry depended on Richmond and Colmore recommending that this should be authorised. The Certificate was handed to the Captain of R.101 in time for the flight.

In addition to the officers and crew who boarded the airship there were six passengers and six officials. Among the former were Lord Thomson and Sir William Sefton Brancker, Director of Civil Aviation. Colmore, Richmond and Scott were three of the officials.

Scott was in uniform and was heard to say: "I am officer in command of the flight . . . I decide such matters as when the ship shall depart, her speed and the height at which she will fly. The Captain of the flight (Irwin) is responsible . . . for carrying out my orders."

This was not what had been arranged. Scott's speech was slurred following a convivial lunch with two members of the crew in Bedford.

To save weight there were severe restrictions on the individual's baggage allowance. The crew members were limited to 10 lbs. Lord Thomson arrived with two cabin trunks, four suitcases, two cases of champagne and a Persian carpet 10 feet long.

A not unfavourable weather forecast proved to be too optimistic when at 6.00 pm there were flurries of rain and a blustery wind. When R.101 set off ninety minutes later the rain was heavy and the wind had strengthened. Large rigid airships had to cruise at low levels to maintain "lift." In turbulent conditions they were liable to be carried up or down as much as 300 feet. R.101 circled over Bedford for almost twenty minutes before setting course. All five engines were running at fast cruise. The air was turbulent; the airship had never flown in worse weather. Irwin and his second in command, Atherstone, must have considered the advisability of returning to the mooring mast. It would not have been in character for Scott to agree. In darkness and in such foul weather mooring would have presented great difficulties. The decision was taken to continue as planned.

Even before the south coast was crossed an engine was shut down on two occasions owing to a drop in oil pressure, for a total period of four hours. Meanwhile a forecast of steadily worsening weather conditions over France was received. The wind was reported to be rising up to 50 mph with strong gusts. Three hours after leaving Cardington and flying at 800 feet R.101 crossed the coast near Hastings. Soon after this all five engines were running again. There is no evidence to suggest that the crew were particularly worried, but they must have been very tired. Scott, Irwin, Atherstone and Johnston completed their watch and went to bed, leaving Flying Officer Steff in charge.

Seven hours into the flight the airship was in the vicinity of Beauvais when it went into a steep dive and struck the ground. Within two minutes there was a series of explosions and R.101 was blazing fiercely. Six of the 54 on board survived to give evidence to accident investigators. The nation was stunned by the tragedy, reminiscent of the sinking of the "Titanic" on her maiden voyage to the United States. But whereas other ocean liners continued to cross the Atlantic, the British government speedily abandoned all further airship endeavour, and R.100 was broken up and sold for scrap.

The conclusion of the accident investigators was that a long rent had probably developed in one of the gasbags in the forward area of R.101. Possibly this had happened because the outer cover had failed in that region, exposing the gasbags to the full force of the airflow of over 50 knots. Subsequently other interested parties pursued their own enquiries and it is possible to offer a reasonably accurate account of the airship's last minutes.

As Scott and other officers finished their watch, Squadron Leader Rope, assistant to Colmore, decided to check the upper surface of the outer cover, aft of the airship's nose. This area had borne the brunt of the heavy rain and the stress of all five engines at full speed. Rope would have known that the outer cover had not been entirely replaced, some parts simply strengthened with stuck-on fabric bands. The decision by Steff, in charge in the control car, to release water ballast and to reduce speed from fast cruise to slow, must have been the result of a warning from Rope of the damage that he had observed.

There was not time for water ballast to be released but the airship stabilised for a few moments. Then with minimal power, hardly any forward speed and no dynamic lift, she dived again and struck the ground. A row of calcium flares was slung along the side of the control car; these were used to observe drift when dropped into the sea. On impact with the wet ground they split and ignited. The two forward engine cars beneath the hull were crushed into it; their exhaust pipes ignited the mixture of air and hydrogen.

"*The Times*" was able to report an interview with one of the survivors, a Mr Disley:

"'I heard a crash and a series of explosions. There were blinding flashes all around, and the next thing I knew was that the ship was on fire. She flared up in an instant, from stem to stern, and I cannot tell how the fire started, but I think it began amidships rather than in the bows.

The fire was awful – awful. It is impossible to describe it. It was just one mass of flame, roaring like a furnace. I threw myself at the fabric cover and tried to break through, but could not. Then I sat down' – one can imagine him crouching under the flames, trying to collect his wits – 'and I found myself sitting in wet grass. I was under the airship, you understand, and the fabric was already torn where I sat. So I crawled along on the ground following the tear, until I found myself outside. I went along to see if I could get anybody out. It was all over in a minute.'

A Frenchman found Mr Disley wandering by the wreck and took him away. Mr Disley would not go to hospital until he had telephoned the Air Ministry and done all he could to summon help."

Following the disaster all those involved with R.100 lost their jobs. Barnes Wallis had already resumed his work on geodetic structure with Vickers and took a prominent part in the construction of the Wellington bomber. He was also responsible for designing the bouncing bomb used to attack the Möhne and Eder dams during the War.

Nevil Shute Norway also returned to the aircraft industry and was one of the founders of Airspeed, best known for the twin-engined Oxford trainer. He continued to write popular novels and his own autobiography, "Slide Rule."

CHAPTER 18

THE BERLIN AIRLIFT

A CITY SAVED FROM STARVATION

In May 1995 most of those who celebrated the fiftieth anniversary of victory in Europe had forgotten the swift onset of the "Cold War" that followed the German surrender. At that time an over-reaction by Russia or the Western Allies might have precipitated another major conflict.

Mr Churchill had tried to persuade General Eisenhower to occupy Berlin before the Russians had reached the city. The latter declined, declaring Berlin to be no more than a geographical location. As a result the Allies had to be content with their own separate sectors in the city, surrounded on all sides by territory under Soviet control. Initially they had access by road, rail, river and three agreed air corridors.

After forcing each one of the East European states to accept Communist governments Russia was ready to try and drive the Allies out of Berlin. On 23rd June 1948 Marshal Sokolovsky declared that, from midnight, road, rail and canal traffic to and from the western sectors of the city would no longer be permitted. No food would be delivered from the Soviet sector nor would coal or electric power continue to be supplied. The pretext for this draconian measure was the introduction by the Allies of new currency to check the rampant inflation caused by the unrestricted circulation of worthless banknotes printed in the eastern sector.

"*The Times*" reported as follows:

"SEVERED WESTERN LINKS WITH BERLIN
SOVIET CHALLENGE TO THE POWERS
MACHINE-GUN POSTS MANNED IN BRITISH SECTOR

The latest Russian restrictions in Berlin are interpreted as a challenge to the continued presence of the western Powers in the city. General Clay, the American Military Governor, has stated that supply by air, on which the western sectors are now entirely dependent, is not possible 'as a long-term policy.'

At the Lehrte station in Berlin last night British troops were setting up barricades and machine-gun posts against a threat of Soviet interference in the British sector."

Over two million Germans lived in West Berlin. Although the Western Governments had become accustomed to continuous provocation they had never anticipated that the Russians would be prepared to subject the civilian population to death by starvation or by freezing in the winter weather. The only remaining way to supply the western sectors of the city was by air. The Russians had agreed to the three corridors to the Allied sectors. They were 20 miles wide and in effect from ground level to 10,000 feet.

Urgent discussions between President Truman and Prime Minister Atlee brought a swift decision to mount an airlift. This was despite the fact that the Joint Chief of Staff did not believe that it would be possible to sustain two million civilians for any length of time. It was estimated that 5,000 tons of coal, food and other necessities were consumed every day. The R.A.F. possessed about 40 Douglas Dakotas and the first squadron of these was despatched to Wunstorf. The Americans could muster about 100 Dakotas but no longer had any of the larger four-engined Douglas Skymasters in Europe; these were hastily summoned from their bases in the Caribbean, Hawaii and Alaska. A Skymaster could carry three times the load of a Dakota. So too could an R.A.F. Avro York and these also were despatched to Germany.

While these larger aircraft were being assembled the U.S.A.F. sent the first of 32 flights of Dakotas from Wiesbaden to Tempelhof on the 26th June; they carried milk, flour and medicines. On 30th June the Skymasters arrived in Germany, loaded cargo at Wiesbaden and Rhein-Main and flew along the southern air corridor to Tempelhof in the American sector of West Berlin. This was a prewar civil airfield, already covered by pierced steel planking (PSP). Radar was available for a ground-controlled approach (GCA) in poor visibility or a low cloud base. A seven-storey building alongside the approach path presented a serious hazard. Living accommodation in Berlin was too scarce for demolition to be an acceptable option. A smokestack rising to 400 feet on the airfield perimeter offered an extra danger to aircraft.

The British bases for delivery flights were Wünstorf, Fassberg, Lübeck, Fühlsbutel, Schleswigland and Finkenwerder. Wunstorf had been built in 1934 and possessed two concrete runways but the main surface was all grass, too easily churned into mud by heavy aircraft. When the Yorks arrived in July PSP was laid down. Fassberg also required PSP to take the Skymasters and the Dakotas were moved to Lubeck. During July R.A.F. Sunderlands and three Aquila Airways Hythes arrived at Finkenwerder on the Elbe.

In the British sector of West Berlin Gatow was covered by PSP. A concrete runway was under construction and was completed a few weeks after the airlift began. GCA was available. R.A.F. aircraft were also equipped with the Blind Approach Beam System (BABS) and Rebecca receivers showing the aircraft's distance from the airfield. The flying boats with their great capacity delivered their loads to the lake Havel See in West Berlin. The French sector of the city did not possess an airfield until Tegel was constructed to take the overload of airlift traffic. It was finished, complete with GCA and BABS, in November.

To back up the British effort 25 private companies contributed 104 civil aircraft. The first to arrive, in July, were several Lancastrians belonging to Alan Cobham's Flight Refuelling Ltd; these were fitted as tankers to carry petrol. They were followed by 10 Dakotas, 6 Yorks, 13 Haltons (converted Halifax bombers), 4 Vikings, 2 Wayfarers and a Liberator.

A number of problems had to be surmounted before the civil aircraft could be integrated into the operation. The private companies used different radio frequencies from the R.A.F., making it necessary to change the crystals in their sets. The Air Licensing Board had to be badgered for several weeks before the aircraft were permitted to carry as heavy a load as an air force machine of the same type. Many arrived in Germany without navigation equipment such as Rebecca. Without this aid they would have been restricted to visual flight conditions. The R.A.F. had to be persuaded to supply them.

There were insufficient spares for both old and new aircraft. None were designed for short trips at maximum weight nor for non-stop operation. The engines of transport aircraft are designed for lengthy periods of cruising. Airframes and undercarriages suffered damage from repeated landings at maximum weight. Coal dust clogged and corroded electrical parts and flying controls.

The British system for despatching aircraft was for the Dakotas to fly to Berlin at 3,000 feet and return from Gatow at 4,500 feet. The Yorks flew to the city at 1,500 feet and returned at 2,500 feet. In bad weather the Dakotas were grounded to avoid the risk of collision if overtaken by the faster Yorks. Three out of every five tons of cargo carried to Berlin was in the form of coal. The city needed 3,000 tons of coal every day for industry, and very little could be spared for domestic use. Electricity could only be supplied for four hours each day and the supply of gas was limited to half of what had been available before the blockade. Shortage of power caused 148 firms to cease trading.

The Berliners had suffered so much bombing during the war that many of them saw themselves as pawns in a conflict between Russia and the Western Powers. They wondered whether the new sacrifices expected of them would not make their lives worse than living under communist rule. But as the pace of the airlift was stepped up and a stream of aircraft was observed to be flying to and from the city, both by day and by night, their hopes were raised by the increasing possibility that the airlift might succeed in its purpose. When the lives of airmen were lost in the inevitable crashes that occurred Berliners were not slow to express their sorrow, their respect and genuine appreciation of the efforts to keep them free of communist domination. In the course of the airlift there were 16 fatal accidents.

The Russians were determined to take all steps short of war to impede the flow of supplies to Berlin. At night they tried to dazzle the pilots with searchlights and sent aircraft above the corridors to drop flares. By day fighters, singly or in formation, flew head-on at the approaching aircraft before pulling up sharply at the last moment. Another tactic was for fighters to dive just ahead of the Berlin-bound stream, firing their cannon as they did so. Radio frequencies used by the Allies were regularly jammed.

Apart from these unwelcome distractions the routine of flying to and from Berlin, all day and every day, including the night, was soul-destroying in its monotony. The American General Turner, appointed to command the airlift, found that some crews left their aircraft when they were being unloaded at Tempelhof to smoke and gossip in a snack bar; they were in no hurry to make the return flight. He gave orders that crews were to remain with their aircraft but arranged for the German Red Cross to hire attractive young women to drive mobile canteens that met each incoming aircraft.

In September Air Vice Marshal Bennett, former Chief Executive of British South American Airways, arrived in Wunstorf with 10 tons of dehydrated potatoes in an Avro Tudor. He acquired a second Tudor and fitted out both as tankers to carry diesel oil. The speed with which the oil could be pumped in and out of the Tudors containers enabled him to make a greater number of trips to the city. By the end of September there were sufficient four-engined aircraft in service for the Americans to phase out all their Dakotas.

In October two squadrons of Handley Page Hastings aircraft arrived at Schleswigland, replacing the civil Dakotas. These new aircraft, which carried the same load as a York, were fitted with a tailwheel and not a tricycle undercarriage. The reason for this was because the cargo door was built to meet a military requirement for the height to match the tailgate of a 15 cwt truck.

As winter set in so did fog. At Gatow the GCA team successfully brought in 1,316 aircraft in the space of 30 days. Ice formation on the Elbe and the Havel See caused the withdrawal from Germany of the flying boats. Tegel was ready to receive aircraft in November and became the principal terminal for the tankers carrying diesel, kerosene and petrol. There was a transmission tower used by the Soviet-controlled Berlin radio station located dangerously close to Tegel's airfield, but the Russians ignored repeated requests for it to be dismantled and moved. Before the year's end the French commandant destroyed it by dynamite; it was one way of celebrating the fact that 100,000 flights had been made successfully to Berlin.

Early in 1949 five Avro Tudors belonging to British South American Airways, each one fitted as a tanker, joined the airlift. B.S.A.A. had lost a second Tudor over the South Atlantic, without trace and for no known reason. The airline had been obliged to withdraw them from the carriage of passengers. The heating system and the pressurisation system were both under suspicion, but as neither was essential on the short low-level flights along the air corridors the Air Registration Board cleared the Tudors for use as freighters; they performed extremely well in this role.

Even before the end of the winter it was apparent that the airlift was proving to be a success, both for the Berliners and, in political terms, for the Western Allies. By the middle of February a million tons had reached Berlin. Early in April Tempelhof GCA handled an aircraft every four minutes over a period of six hours. The 21st April was the 300th day of the blockade and, as if to show the Russians that the airlift would continue indefinitely, construction of a third runway at Gatow was begun.

On 12th May 1949 the Russians admitted defeat by lifting the blockade. The Berliners were able to give a rapturous reception to a long procession of trucks which rolled along the autobahn into the city. Over 2,300,000 tons had been flown into Berlin. Accidents to aircraft had caused the deaths of 31 American and 29 British airmen. Given the punishing schedule demanded of the pilots it is remarkable that the accident rate was not much higher. Air Vice Marshal Bennett had flown two or three sorties into Berlin every night for six months, a feat which was described in the official report as "an epic of human endeavour that can have few parallels in the history of aviation."

CHAPTER 19

THE AVRO TUDOR

ONE MAN'S STRUGGLE TO PROVE ITS WORTH

In 1939 the outbreak of war interrupted any hopes that the British Overseas Airways Corporation could look forward to the provision of a British-manufactured landplane to replace its aged Handley Page HP.42s. The armed struggle was still continuing when in 1944 the Air Ministry presented A.V. Roe with the specification for an airliner able to carry sixty passengers at 235 mph and 25,000 feet across the North Atlantic.

A.V. Roe had built the highly-regarded Lancaster bomber and Roy Chadwick, the chief designer, was given the task of producing a successful airliner. In November 1944 the Ministry of Supply ordered a dozen Tudor Is and the prototype made its first flight in June 1945. Yet B.O.A.C. was never consulted about its own requirements in regard to range and payload, whilst A.V. Roe was instructed by the Ministry not to deal directly with their intended customer.

When it was realised that the Tudor would be able to carry only twelve passengers across the Atlantic A.V. Roe agreed to extend the fuselage by six feet and to provide accommodation for 28 passengers. Meanwhile Lockheed was receiving orders for the proven Constellation L-049 and Douglas was not far behind with their DC-6.

In March 1946 the extended Tudor made its maiden flight, but the tropical trials conducted in Nairobi later that year convinced B.O.A.C. that the aircraft was totally unsuitable to their African and Indian routes, let alone the North Atlantic. Both Quantas and South African Airways also lost interest and bought American airliners. A.V. Roe's problems were further compounded when Roy Chadwick and test pilot S. Thorn were killed testing a Tudor.

Meanwhile British South American Airways was operating "stopgap" military derivatives, Lancastrians and Yorks. The chief executive was Air Vice Marshal Don Bennett who had led Bomber Command's Pathfinder Force; he was determined to fly British-built aircraft. Subject to the result of tropical trials conducted by himself, and at a greatly reduced price, he was prepared to consider the Tudor IV, powered by Rolls Royce Merlin 623 engines.

A deal was done and in August 1947 Bennett set off for Jamaica with a refuelling stop at Gander. Over the Atlantic a fuel feed problem developed, with a real possibility that the aircraft might have to be ditched. An emergency was declared and rescue services alerted. Fortunately the engines continued to run and Gander was reached. On landing it was discovered that a fuel service cock, not accessible in flight, had been left in the shut position.

The tropical trials were carried out to Bennett's satisfaction and he declared the Tudor to be a better aircraft than the Constellation. A number of the rejected Tudor Is were required for crew training pending deliveries of the Tudor IV. Although this was their first experience of a pressurised airliner the airline's pilots were not greatly impressed by its handling or performance. The manufacturers had not fitted a tricycle undercarriage. The massive tail made it difficult for the pilot to keep the aircraft on the runway in gusty crosswind conditions, particularly if the runway surface was covered with a layer of ice or compacted snow. The cabin heater often failed in flight, requiring a swift descent to avoid freezing everyone on board. This procedure often brought the aircraft into cloud, whereupon ice formed on the wings. When stars were visible in the night sky the lack of an astrodome was unhelpful to navigation.

Notwithstanding these inconveniences a Tudor carried commercial passengers for the first time in September 1947. Their destination was Chile and the following month witnessed the inaugural service of the aircraft to the Caribbean. On 27th January 1948 *"Star Tiger"* left Heathrow for Bermuda via Lisbon and the Azores. Problems were encountered early on, the heater failing at 21,000 feet. Compass trouble and an engine snag were remedied at Lisbon, but the heater again failed on the way to the Azores. *"Star Tiger"* reported nothing untoward on the long flight to Bermuda, having chosen to cruise at 2,000 feet to combat strong headwinds at higher flight levels. The last radio message from the aircraft was received when it was within 200 miles of the island. Thereafter repeated calls from Bermuda were not answered. Searching aircraft found no trace of wreckage and the cause of this sudden disaster could not be determined.

At home the response of the Air Registration Board was to advise the Minister of Civil Aviation, Lord Nathan, to ground the Tudor, pending an investigation. Bennett protested that there was no shred of evidence to suggest that the aircraft was unsafe to fly. A boardroom row erupted and he left the company. But very soon afterwards events brought Bennett and the Tudor together again. The Russians imposed a land blockade on Berlin and the Western Allies responded with an airlift of every transport aircraft which they could muster; this had to include civil machines.

Bennett bought two Tudors from A.V. Roe and founded his own company, Airflight. The A.R.B. certified these to fly as freighters, unpressurised. In any case the air corridors into Berlin were flown at a low level. The first load, which Bennett flew himself, was ten tons of potatoes. Initially Airflight's one other pilot was only licensed for daylight flying, so Bennett flew three round trips to Berlin every night. In October 1948 his two Tudors were converted to carry almost ten tons of diesel oil. This was the heaviest load of any aircraft being operated on the airlift.

The investigation into the airworthiness of the Tudor had found no dangerous characteristics and B.S.A.A. had resumed passenger flights. Two Tudors were employed on the airlift, converted into tankers. But in January 1949, in circumstances as mysterious as had arisen before, "Star Ariel" disappeared without trace. No warning of trouble had been transmitted since the aircraft had departed Bermuda. The Tudor was cruising towards Nassau in daylight and in perfect weather. Once again B.S.A.A. was obliged to withdraw its fleet from passenger service.

These two disasters effectively ended the existence of the company but Bennett refused to accept that the Tudor possessed any serious defect and attributed their fate to sabotage. His own company had operated 977 return flights to Berlin and earned substantial profits. When the Russians lifted the blockade of Berlin in August 1949 Bennett's Tudors were converted to carry passengers and various modifications recommended by the A.R.B.

were carried out. The aircraft were then certified to carry up to 78 passengers. He continued operations under a new title, Fairflight. The first charter, to carry apprentices to England, was obtained from the government of Pakistan. Other contracts followed, to Johannesburg, to Japan and 25 round trips between Aden and Israel.

Then it was Bennett's company which suffered a tragic accident, although the probable cause was less mysterious. The Tudor, bringing Rugby football supporters back from Dublin to a small airfield in Wales, crashed on the final approach. 75 passengers and five crew members were killed. It was known that the pilot had expressed unease about the short length of the runway. Witnesses to the accident described what appeared to be a stall as the Tudor was about to land.

Bennett continued to obtain contracts for the remaining Tudor. Flights to supply stores to the British troops in Korea were followed by freight services between Hamburg and Berlin.

In November 1951 he sold Fairflight to another entrepreneur who clearly shared his confidence in the Tudor. Freddie Laker had founded Air Charter Limited in 1947 and conducted *ad hoc* operations from Croydon. By taking over Fairflight he inherited the contract to carry freight from Berlin. Recognising the great capacity of the Tudor he bought all those that remained on the market. These were four Tudor Is, two Mark IIIs and four Mark IVs. A very thorough conversion programme was carried out, including the installation of a huge freight door.

Renamed the Supertrader the aircraft was granted a full C. of A. in February 1954 and the maximum all-up weight was increased to 83,600 lbs. In a test identical to that undertaken by the A.R.B. in 1946 the aircraft was found to perform far better. Laker's Supertraders were engaged in trooping to the Middle and Far East. A colonial coach service was also operated to Libya and Nigeria. Freight services were also flown for the British government to the Woomera rocket range in Australia. In every configuration the Supertraders performed extremely well and were not withdrawn from service until 1959.

If B.O.A.C. had been involved in the Tudor's development from the beginning, and if the two disasters over the Western Atlantic had not taken place, could the Tudor have become a more successful airliner? One handicap was the failure to provide the aircraft with a tricycle undercarriage. Designed in wartime, A.V. Roe had used the wings and undercarriage of their Lincoln, the successor to the Lancaster. Four-engined airliners with a tailwheel no longer featured in the production of the major American manufacturers. At home Vickers were the first to produce a turbine powered airliner, the Viscount. De Havilland led the world with the first pure-jet passenger airliner, the Comet. A new era had begun, ushered in by the rapid advance of technology as a consequence of wartime priorities.

CHAPTER 20

THE HANDLEY PAGE HERMES:

NOBODY'S FAVOURITE AIRLINER

In 1936 the British government's belated recognition of Germany's military ambitions had resulted in top priority being given to the production of bombers and fighters to the exclusion of civil aircraft. Consequently plans for a modern airliner suitable for international routes existed only on drawing boards. With the end of the war the British Overseas Airways Corporation had been obliged to use the Avro Lancastrian, a converted bomber, and its derivative the York, on its African and Eastern services. The Short flying boats were costing more each year to operate than they could earn in revenue.

To permit B.O.A.C. to compete on equal terms on the North Atlantic route the government had authorised the expenditure of scarce dollars for the purchase of Lockheed Constellations. In addition the airline was also supplied with 22 of the Canadian-built Douglas DC-4M, a pressurised version of the successful Skymaster, but powered by Rolls Royce Merlin engines. Known as the Argonaut class these entered service in July 1949.

Handley Page had been keen to produce a large airliner for a number of years but the ordering of aircraft was then the responsibility of the Air Ministry, not B.O.A.C. Only when the shortcomings of A.V. Roe's Tudor, the ministry's original choice, became apparent did Handley Page receive any encouragement and finally an order for about two dozen Hermes. This aircraft owed its origins to their Hastings military transport, but it was built with a tricycle undercarriage.

B.O.A.C. had accepted the Constellation and Argonaut "off the peg" but was determined to be involved in the development of Handley Page's airliner. The Argonaut had been equipped with one nosewheel-steering tiller, but a second (for the co-pilot) was demanded on the Hermes. Relations with the Bristol company which manufactured the Hercules engines were less than harmonious. An ongoing problem with propeller overspeeding soured dealings with de Havilland.

In early trials of the prototype Hermes tailplane flutter was encountered and a strong pull on the elevators was required to get the tail down for the landing. Such difficulties, not unusual in the development phase, could be overcome but the unexpectedly high basic weight of the aircraft, inevitably diminishing the hoped-for payload, resulted in the refusal of B.O.A.C. to accept the first six machines to come off the production line. Another cause for dissatisfaction stemmed from the incidence of the aerofoil section. With power selected for the economical cruise condition there was both engine and airframe vibration. This could be avoided by applying more power but at the expense of increased fuel consumption and reduced engine life.

When the Hermes was cruised at lesser power and lower airspeed its pronounced nose-up attitude incurred a penalty in icing conditions; as much ice formed under the leading edge of the aerofoil as above it. With deliveries thus delayed it was not until July 1950 that B.O.A.C. accepted their first aircraft. This was named *"Hannibal"* after a famous predecessor of the HP.42 class which had entered service in 1931. Captain A.S.M. Rendall, who had flown as a co-pilot on the HP.42, was appointed Flight Superintendent and was present at the naming ceremony performed by Lord Pakenham, Minister for Civil Aviation. The Hermes replaced the York on the route to West Africa in August and in November took over the East African service from the Short Solent flying boats which were retired.

Eventually 20 Hermes were accepted, the last in January 1951. It is only fair to record that the aircraft had a pressurisation and air-conditioning system, complete with humidifiers, as good as any American airliner then flying and better than most. It also introduced the first AC electrical system on a British aircraft. In the original 40-seat passenger configuration prior to tourist or military additions, both space and comfort were excellent. The crew compartment was also spacious and needed to be. Two pilots, a navigator, flight engineer and radio operator had to be accommodated. Originally an astrodome had been fitted; then a Constellation so equipped had suffered a fracture and the loss of the navigator, so the astrodome was removed and an aperture for a periscopic sextant substituted.

B.O.A.C. remained very disappointed with the payload and high operating costs of the Hermes. Their withdrawal from service was planned to coincide with the introduction of de Havilland's Comet 1 on the South African route in May 1952. Prior to that date a Hermes suffered damage when the propeller and reduction gear of an inboard engine broke away and knocked a large hole in the fuselage, injuring a crew member. The aircraft landed safely in Tripoli. On another occasion an outer propeller struck the inner engine before flying over the fuselage. When B.O.A.C. began to retire the Hermes Handley Page had built a total of 26 and received no further orders. By the end of March 1953 only nine Hermes remained on the African service, others being sold or cocooned to await disposal.

The opportunity afforded to the British independent airlines to buy a four-engined pressurised airliner under three years old and at a greatly reduced price was too good to miss. Airwork Limited had previously obtained a contract for trooping flights using Douglas Dakotas and Vickers Vikings. In 1952 six Hermes were purchased and a seventh in 1957. With a new contract to ferry troops to the Egyptian canal zone and to Kenya, Airwork carried out its own tropical trials and decided to derate the engines to accept the lower-octane fuel more easily obtainable at many of the airliner's destinations. An additional generator was fitted together with hydraulic locks to prevent the propellers overspeeding.

In July 1952 an Airwork Hermes made a crash-landing near Orleans when the starboard outer propeller detached itself and struck the inner propeller. Fortunately there were no injuries to sixty or more of those on board. The following month a Hermes en route to Khartoum was forced to ditch off Sicily when two propellers began overspeeding in quick succession. There were several fatalities among the passengers. Airwork suffered no further accidents arising from this cause and claimed to be obtaining 2,400 hours each year from each Hermes. This was considered to be both creditable and profitable.

166

The grounding of the Comet 1 following the crash at Elba merely delayed B.O.A.C.'s complete withdrawal of the Hermes while the airline searched for second-hand Constellations. In 1954 Britavia Limited bought five Hermes from B.O.A.C. to fulfil a trooping contract. The aircraft needed work done to them before they could be flown to their new owner's base at Blackbushe but B.O.A.C.'s engineers refused to carry this out; they feared a loss of their own jobs. Britavia threatened B.O.A.C. with a writ before the situation was resolved. In addition to trooping, ad hoc charters were undertaken and a Hermes, in Britavia's colours, was seen for the first time in New York.

In 1959, with Blackbushe airport about to be closed, the Hermes fleet was transferred to Manston in Kent to be operated by an associated company, Silver City. This airline had been responsible for the construction of an airport called Ferryfield, near Dungeness, where a car ferry service to France had proved successful. Ferryfield possessed too short a runway for the Hermes so Manston became the starting point for a "Silver Arrow" passenger service to Le Touquet. Silver City continued to operate the Hermes on both trooping flights and inclusive tours until the end of 1962.

In September 1954 Skyways Limited bought from B.O.A.C. the first of a dozen Hermes for use on inclusive tours and trooping flights. This was the company's first pressurised aircraft, having previously used Yorks. Seating was provided for 68 passengers. Skyways used the Hermes on their scheduled passenger service between Heathrow and Tunis.

In January 1960 two Hermes were transferred to Bahamas Airways in which Skyways had an interest. But with seating increased to carry 78 passengers on the short sectors from Nassau to Fort Lauderdale and West Palm Beach it proved difficult to attract custom. Losses multiplied. The final straw was the alarming occasion when on take-off an outer propeller flew into the inner engine propeller before tearing through the nose of the aircraft. The Hermes were flown back to England and Skyways sold three to Air Safaris Limited in 1961. This company ceased operations in 1962 following failure to raise sufficient funds.

Falcon Airways operated one Hermes on charters between 1959 and 1961. The solitary Hermes of Air Links, G-ALDA, was the last Hermes to fly commercially.

The Handley Page Hermes flew in the service of its various owners for a span of about a dozen years from its introduction in the summer of 1950. That is not a long time in comparison with other airliners but very much longer than the two years during which B.O.A.C. took the decision to withdraw it, blaming high operating costs and the poor payload. Once the airline had accepted delivery of the first of the 20 Hermes, any call for modifications to the engines, propellers, electrical equipment or anything else obviously incurred extra expense and every new aircraft is found to need modifications: the Hermes was no exception.

It must be remembered that B.O.A.C. was top-heavy with office staff. The same situation existed in the maintenance areas where the unions employed restrictive practices and resisted any flexibility in the allocation of work. In the private sector both management and employees were keenly aware that any work offered to them by the government was work which B.O.A.C. was not in a position to undertake. Scheduled services were very rarely allocated to the independent companies, whilst currency restrictions imposed by the Treasury hampered holiday travel. They operated on a very tight budget indeed and their employees were well aware of it.

At a time when the nation was still suffering severely from the financial costs of the recent war the independent airlines were never able to buy new modern American airliners – seldom, second-hand ones. Consequently the first home-produced pressurised four-engined airliner with a tricycle undercarriage was "Hobson's Choice." At a bargain price with as many seats as could be crammed into the fuselage a modest profit could be made.

Moreover, as experience was gained in the operation of new equipment, solutions to earlier problems were found and recurring snags usually eliminated by modifications or mode of usage. Mandatory times between overhaul of engines and equipment were extended, reducing the time aircraft spent in the hangar, unavailable for earning revenue.

The government's trooping contracts provided the bread and butter for the independent operators of the Hermes. Later, as overseas bases were abandoned, inclusive tours to Mediterranean and other foreign resorts were made possible by the easing of currency restrictions. These opportunities brought much-needed revenue. But, in retrospect, how many pilots or passengers can look back upon the Hermes as their favourite airliner?

CHAPTER 21

THE COMET 1:

THE WORLD'S FIRST JET AIRLINER

Forty years ago several mysterious disasters interrupted jet airline services for a further four years.

In 1944, even before the war was won, a committee chaired by Lord Brabazon of Tara took steps to encourage British aircraft manufacturers to re-enter the civil airliner market, which was dominated by American piston-engined machines. Great Britain led the world in jet propulsion systems and the intention was to leapfrog current technology and to establish a commanding lead with a new generation of pure-jet airliners.

The de Havilland company and the British Overseas Airways Corporation were keen to follow this course. But whilst the Brabazon committee envisaged a jet mail courier for the North Atlantic as a first step, Sir Frederick de Havilland and B.O.A.C. were more interested in a passenger aircraft, with mail taking second place. The Air Ministry, which controlled the purse strings, ordered 24 machines. The name Comet was revived; the original twin-engined aircraft bearing this name had won the Mildenhall-to-Melbourne air race of 1934.

Construction began at Hatfield in complete secrecy. The head of the design team, Ronald Bishop, chose the de Havilland Ghost engine which had been proved on the company's Venom fighters. Because this was a 'fat' engine likely to cause considerable drag Bishop decided to bury the four Ghost engines in the wing rather than in pods. By 1947 the general layout of the Comet was agreed, an all-metal aircraft with an operating crew of four and seating 36 passengers. It was designed for a safe life of 30,000 flying hours. Two prototypes were built and the first of these was flown by the company's chief test pilot, John Cunningham, in July 1949.

Designed to operate stage lengths of 1,500 miles at just under 500 mph the Comet consumed fuel at twice the rate of a piston-engined airliner. However its far greater speed, almost double that of the latter, made the cost per ton-mile and passenger-mile competitive. By flying nearly 50% more ton-miles or passenger-miles per year five Comets could do the work of eight piston-engined aircraft. The passenger cabin was considerably quieter than those of conventional airliners and vibration was negligible. With a ceiling of 40,000 feet the Comet could usually cruise above ice-bearing and turbulent clouds. As no other civil aircraft was flying at this level air traffic control problems were seldom encountered; as with today's Concorde the Comet could expect a landing clearance without delay.

The auguries were all favourable when, on May 2nd 1952, the first commercial service left Heathrow for Johannesburg and covered 6,700 miles in under 24 hours. In August Ceylon came on-line and Singapore in October. Orders for Comet 1s were placed by Air France and the Royal Canadian Air Force. A longer-range Comet 2 was in production and orders came in from Panair do Brasil, Japan Air Lines and Linea Aerea Venezolana. A Comet 3 with Rolls Royce Avon engines and a transatlantic range was planned. Pan-American Airways and Air India were among those placing orders.

It is not at all uncommon for newly-introduced airliners to pose problems for flight crews. In October 1952 a B.O.A.C. Comet began its take-off run from Rome's Ciampino airport. It was a dark night and there was no visible horizon. Rain was falling. The captain was a very experienced pilot who had been an instructor on previous aircraft which he had flown. It was in his nature to fly strictly according to the training manual.

This called for the nosewheel to be lifted at 80 knots and when the speed increased to 112 knots to 'unstick' and begin the climb. At 112 knots he eased back the control column. The Comet immediately stalled and bounced on the runway. The captain closed the throttles to abandon the take-off but the aircraft overshot the runway and suffered damage beyond the boundary lights. There were no fatalities or serious injuries.

An examination of the runway revealed scrape-marks caused by the tail-skid. A court of enquiry decreed that the captain had made an error of judgement in failing to appreciate that he had raised the nose of the aircraft too high on take-off. He was taken off Comets and, to avoid dismissal, accepted the blame. Thereafter he was employed flying the company's oldest York aircraft, carrying freight. Five months later a Comet of Canadian Pacific Airlines failed to become airborne on a night take-off from Karachi airport. The pilot was another very experienced former training captain who had previously flown for Imperial Airways and B.O.A.C. Once again the runway showed scrape-marks made by the tail-skid. All those on board the Comet perished in the fire that followed the crash.

B.O.A.C. saw the need to revise the take-off drill and pilots were instructed to keep the nosewheel on the ground until the speed reached 112 knots. But this caused 'hammering' and de Havilland disapproved, fearing weakening of metal in the nosewheel area. John Cunningham conducted tests, deliberately raising the nose too high. It was accepted that in conditions of high weight and temperature, when no visual horizon was apparent, the artificial horizon on the pilot's instrument panel provided an inadequate indication of nose-up angle. Moreover the tests showed that the stalling speed near the ground was higher than the corresponding figure in free air. As the aircraft weight increased so did the disparity in stalling speed.

De Havilland acknowledged that these ground stalls were caused by the Comet's aerofoil section not having been designed for a high angle of attack. To prevent any more take-off accidents resulting from the nose being raised too high, a drooped leading edge to the wing was introduced and all Comets were modified. Unfortunately this came too late for the B.O.A.C. captain who had been dismissed from flying jets. After months spent attempting to salvage his professional reputation he died of a heart attack.

In April a Comet service to Tokyo was introduced. This achieved 89% load factors and in May the first year of jet operations ended with 80% of capacity offered in terms of seats and cargo space being sold.

Sadly May also witnessed B.O.A.C.'s first Comet disaster. G-ALYV would have been concluding a climb from Calcutta when witnesses on the ground heard explosions and saw debris falling from the clouds. The monsoon season had set in and thunderstorms were forecast. Wreckage was found over a very wide area and it was assumed at the time that very severe turbulence, capable of destroying any aircraft, had caused the catastrophe. One result of this event was to focus attention on the need to install storm warning radar in airliners.

Comet operations continued. In July 1953 an aircraft which ran off the runway into soggy ground at Calcutta caused no serious injuries and was repaired. Elsewhere there were several mishaps involving undershooting and resultant heavy landings. These were attributed to the Comet's habit of sinking rapidly if the speed fell off on the final approach. If the speed was kept up the aircraft tended to float during the hold-off. At Entebbe a man standing short of the runway was struck by the landing gear and killed.

In September John Cunningham flew a Comet 2 to South America on a proving and demonstration flight. This was the first time a jet airliner had visited that continent. De Havilland were looking forward to an increasing number of sales when another disaster to a Comet made headlines throughout the world.

Comet G-ALYP, thereafter known as "Yoke Peter," had left Rome for Heathrow on January 10th 1954. In the course of the climb the captain made radio contact with a B.O.A.C. Argonaut which had left Ciampino thirty minutes earlier. The two captains were actually conversing when radio contact was abruptly lost. Moments later fishermen off Elba and residents on the island heard explosions above them and some saw the Comet trailing smoke as it fell towards the sea. On receiving the news Sir Miles Thomas, chairman of B.O.A.C., immediately grounded the entire Comet fleet and a major investigation was set in train.

In addition to the Air Registration Board, the R.A.E. at Farnborough and de Havilland, this involved the Royal Navy and a flotilla of chartered Italian trawlers. B.O.A.C. and de Havilland regarded fire as the most likely cause of the accident following an uncontained engine failure with debris decompressing the fuselage. "Yoke Peter" had made only 1,290 pressurised flights. Before commercial services had begun de Havilland had rigorously tested the pressure cabin structure and windows in an altitude test chamber specially built at Hatfield. The pressure hull had been tested to the equivalent of 16,000 flights before a failure had appeared. The possibility of sabotage was considered; if proved this would have been preferable to the awful possibility that the Comet had not been of sound construction. The airline and aircraft manufacturers had played for very high stakes in the whole venture.

Off Elba Royal Navy vessels, equipped with underwater television, a deep sea diver's observation chamber and special grabs, began the time-consuming process of searching for the engines and sections of the wing and fuselage for despatch to Farnborough. More than a dozen bodies from the aircraft were recovered from the sea and forensic experts were able to declare that none had drowned. All had died instantly as a result of "a violent and explosive decompression."

Meanwhile de Havilland initiated sixty modifications to the Comet, one or more of which it was expected would eliminate the possibility that a similar accident could recur. The main modification upon which most hopes were placed involved armour-plating round the engines to seal them from the passenger cabin and fuel tanks.

The accident to "Yoke Peter" had happened in January. In March de Havilland and B.O.A.C. were satisfied that the modifications which had been completed would make a resumption of Comet services possible. Then on April 8th G-ALYY, en route from Rome to Cairo, exploded and fell into the sea near Naples. "Yoke Yoke" had made under 1,000 pressurised flights.

What followed was inevitable. The certificate of airworthiness was withdrawn and Comet 1 commercial flights ceased for ever. It was a catastrophe for de Havilland, which faced the cancellation of a stream of orders, and a terrible setback for B.O.A.C. which instantly lost 20 per cent of its carrying capacity.

"*The Times*" reported as follows:

> "Mr Lennox Boyd, Minsster of Transport and Civil Aviation, has withdrawn the United Kingdom certificate of airworthiness of all Comet aircraft, pending further detailed investigations into the causes of the recent disasters.
>
> Before doing so he took the advice of the Air Registration Board and the Air Safety Board and discussed the matter with

the Chairman of B.O.A.C. In this decision the manufacturers, the de Havilland companies, fully concur . . .

Wreckage and bodies were sighted in the sea yesterday from a B.E.A. Elizabethan airliner near the area where a large patch of oil, 70 miles due south of Naples, had given the first clue to the probable fate of the B.O.A.C. Comet G-ALYY."

The investigation to discover the cause of the accidents went ahead with renewed urgency. A water tank was constructed at Farnborough in which a Comet was immersed. It was subjected to an accelerated series of tests to check the cabin under repeated cycles of pressurising and depressurising as would occur in normal flight. The wing, projecting through the sides of the tank by means of waterproof seals, was flexed up and down by a row of hydraulic jigs for days on end. Meanwhile 70 per cent of the Elba Comet had been recovered, taken to Farnborough and pieced together on a wooden skeleton frame. All four engines had also been found.

In the course of the water tests the pressure cabin failed. Examination revealed that a rent in the side of the cabin appeared to start from a rivet at the corner of a window frame. After repairs the tests were resumed and a similar failure occurred; once again this had started at the corner of a window frame. De Havilland had designed the cabin to withstand a pressure of up to 20 lbs to the square inch. The investigation established that structural and material strength were not safeguards against metal fatigue. Clearly not enough was then known about this and thereafter much more attention had to be paid to metal fatigue. Ronald Bishop regretted that he had agreed to a production request for the window frame reinforcements to be riveted rather than bonded with Redux metal glue.

Four months after the Naples accident Sir Arnold Hall, director of the R.A.E., presented his findings to the government's Comet enquiry. First and foremost the cabin was found to be weaker than expected and prone to fatigue after a short life. The wing also was prone to fatigue. A fatigue crack, which would have caused the wing to break, had appeared. Manufacturing cracks were found in a highly-stressed area. Some rivets were not inserted in the correct place. Rapid refuelling could damage the outer wing tanks. Fuel that could overflow from the tanks represented a fire hazard. The

Comet did not always handle well on take-off and landing. Finally jet effluxes produced fatigue in the rear fuselage; this happened because at the moment of take-off, as the nose was raised, the forced draught from the engines hit the runway and bounced up against the fuselage. After several hundred take-offs this induced fatigue in the area forward of the tail.

Sir Arnold Hall had brought the technical investigation to a successful conclusion with great efficiency and speed. But Sir Frederick de Havilland was subjected to severe questioning at the subsequent inquiry. Counsel for the passengers, for the pilots and for the navigator and engineer, wanted to know why Sir Frederick was so certain that the modifications to the Comet, adopted after the accident at Elba, had rendered the aircraft safe to fly. Would not a lengthier period of search and investigation have prevented the second accident near Naples? Sir Frederick agreed that over a prolonged period more wreckage might have been found but not necessarily any obvious cause of the crash.

Sir Arnold Hall explained that the water tests at Farnborough had revealed the likely cause. This was confirmed by the fortunate recovery of the metal panel bearing the rent. The wreckage trail might have spread over 20 miles and into much deeper water.

Lord Brabazon was chairman of the Air Registration Board; he had gained the very first civil air pilot's licence to be issued prior to the first World War. In a robust speech he made some controversial points:

"We could not delay flying the Comet for ever . . . you and I know the cause of this accident. It is due to the adventurous pioneering spirit of our race. It has been like that in the past, it is like that in the present and I hope it will be in the future . . . We all went into it with our eyes wide open . . . We did not know what fate was going to hold out for us in the future. Of course we gave hostages to fate but I cannot believe that this court or our country will censure us because we ventured . . . it is metallurgy, not aeronautics, that is in the dock."

The enquiry cleared everyone of blame for the accidents, implicitly acknowledging that progress in an entirely new field of endeavour involved unknown risks and consequences. De Havilland passed on to Boeing everything that they had learned about fatigue. In return Boeing shared its knowledge of podded jets, particularly the drag that they caused. Development of a strengthened and improved Comet went ahead. A new expression "fail-safe" came into use. The fuselage shell of the Comet 4 was constructed 80 per cent thicker than its predecessor. Tougher aluminium alloys were used. Copper alloys replaced zinc alloys. Modifications involved replacing a whole length of window panels with one of increased strength with special reinforcement around all windows, hatches, doors or other openings. Rolls Royce Avon engines would be fitted with jet pipes angled away from the fuselage.

The proceedings of the public enquiry elicited much interest and even admiration around the world.

The *"New York Herald Tribune"* offered "full marks to Britain for its brutally honest and frank enquiry."

"Time" magazine declared: "British science has told the world without excuse or cover-up what happened to their proudest airliner, the ill-starred jet Comet."

Four years later the Comet 4 inaugurated the first jet airliner service across the North Atlantic. But Boeing had their own 707 ready and this was the aeroplane which was to dominate the skies for years to come.

CHAPTER 22

THE MUNICH AIR DISASTER

THE CAUSE DISPUTED

There is a saying amongst airmen that the pilot is the first to arrive at the scene of an aircraft accident. If human error is thought to be the cause then inevitably he becomes the prime suspect. If he has survived to offer his own account of the events leading up to the accident it does not follow that he will not be counted among the victims.

On February 5th 1958 a twin-engined Airspeed Elizabethan, G-ALZU, operated by British European Airways, was returning to England from Belgrade. This was a charter flight bringing home the Manchester United football team that had won through to the final of the European Cup. There were 38 passengers on board including players, club officials and journalists.

B.E.A. had bought 19 Elizabethans. The type had originated in a Brabazon Committee requirement for a Douglas DC-3 replace-ment. Due to development delays they had not entered service until March 1952. By February 1957 they were all put up for sale as a consequence of the very successful introduction of the Vickers Viscount turboprop airliners. Only five Elizabethans had been sold, the remainder being engaged on services to Europe and the Mediterranean.

Munich had been selected as the refuelling stop en route to Manchester. Light snow was falling as the aircraft landed. The runway was observed to be covered with both snow and slush. The depth and importance of these deposits was to become a source of considerable controversy. Whilst the aircraft was being refuelled the outside air temperature was reported to be -0.2°C. Due to the high aspect ratio of the wing the pilot could not obtain a good view of the whole upper surface from the cockpit windows, but from the ground it was observed that melted snow was running off the trailing edge. For this reason the commander, James Thain, did not order the station engineer to have the aircraft deiced.

The co-pilot, Kenneth Rayment, was also a captain and senior to Thain. The two pilots were old friends and Rayment had agreed to fly in the junior capacity. B.E.A. regulations required the commander to occupy the left-hand seat at all times. Thain had flown the outbound sectors to Belgrade and had decided that Rayment should fly the return sectors. As a fully-qualified Elizabethan captain it would be the natural thing for him to do so from the left-hand seat.

One hour after landing at Munich the passengers were boarded and the aircraft was taxied out to the runway. When Rayment opened the throttles to begin the take-off run the tyre tracks of aircraft that had previously landed and taken off were visible in the snow and slush. As the power was increased one of the Bristol Centaurus engines began to surge. Rayment closed the throttles and obtained permission from the control tower to taxy back along the runway for a second attempt. The second take-off run was abandoned for the same reason and the aircraft taxied back to the ramp for an examination by the station engineer. The latter attributed the surging to the height above sea level of the airfield and recommended a throttle adjustment procedure that should eliminate the problem.

Before the aircraft was taxied out for the third time the airport authority routinely examined the runway and estimated the depth of slush to amount to only 1/8th of an inch. It is important to understand that during the 1950s there was no general appreciation by pilots of the magnitude of drag due to slush. Indeed, at that time, aircraft operating manuals barely mentioned the effects of slush on the runway. The very few that recommended caution failed to specify the maximum depth that could be accepted.

When the third take-off run began Thain called out the speed as registered on the airspeed indicator. Rayment looked ahead, keeping the aircraft straight by use of the nosewheel until sufficient airflow existed to use the rudder pedals. The decision speed, known as "V-One" was 117 knots, after which insufficient runway length remained to allow the aircraft to be halted. On achieving that speed Thain called: "V-One." By then the final third of the runway had been reached in an area where previous aircraft had not disturbed the snow and slush. The speed did not continue to rise as Thain had expected but fell off to 105 knots. He pushed the throttles forward to their stops. Rayment lifted the aircraft nose and, hoping to reduce the drag, called for Thain to retract the undercarriage.

The Elizabethan reached the boundary fence and crashed through it. Continuing, it struck a house, and that caused a wing to be torn off, the engine setting fire to the building. The port side of the aircraft hit a tree. The shattered fuselage spun round and demolished a wooden garage. The tailplane broke away but the forward section of the Elizabethan travelled on another 70 yards. By this time many of those on board were already dead and others severely injured.

Thain was unhurt, as was the radio operator who shut off the electrical master switches to avoid any arcing that might set off an explosion. Rayment, trapped in the wreckage, was in a critical condition. The steward was killed but the two stewardesses survived. Among the passengers 21 died and 17 survived. Five weeks later Rayment succumbed to his injuries. Within hours almost every country in the world broadcast the news that the celebrated Manchester United team had suffered a major disaster.

"The Times" reported an account of the crash given by a survivor, the *"Daily Mail"* reporter Peter Howard, who was the only one of the Press party to be well enough to describe the events:

> "It was snowing when we landed at Munich. I was sitting in the front row of seats on the starboard side. When the pilot tried to take off there seemed to be some kind of slight fault with the engines. He stopped.
>
> Then he tried a second take-off. That did not seem satisfactory so he taxied back to the apron to get things checked up. It was on the third take-off that we crashed. I think we were about the end of the runway, only a bit above the ground.
>
> The 'plane suddenly seemed to be breaking up. Seats started to crumble up. Everything seemed to be falling to pieces.

It was a rolling sensation and all sorts of stuff started coming down on top of us. There was not time to think. No one cried out. No one spoke; just a deadly silence for what could only have been seconds. I cannot remember whether there was a bang or not. Everything stopped all at once. I was so dazed I just scrambled about. Then I found a hole in the wreckage and crawled out on hands and knees.

I turned and saw Harry Gregg, the goalkeeper. Gregg, Ted Ellyard, the two stewardesses, the radio officer and myself went back into the wreckage. I saw Captain Thain, one of the crew, start putting out small fires with an extinguisher.

It looked as though those who had been sitting in the forward part of the 'plane were the lucky ones who got out. The luckiest of all were those in backward-facing seats.

Part of the engines of the airliner had gone forward for 150 yards and hit a small house which burst into flames, but the fuselage did not catch fire."

The Queen said in a message to the Minister of Transport and Civil Aviation and to the Lord Mayor of Manchester:

"I am deeply shocked to hear of the accident to the 'plane carrying members of Manchester United Football Club and newspapermen back from Belgrade. Please convey my sympathy and that of my husband to the relatives of those who have been killed and to the injured."

President Tito sent a message to Mr McMillan:

"I am deeply moved by the news of the disaster, which is a heavy blow to English sport and to the English people. Allow me to express my deepest sympathy."

The Red Star Club in Belgrade, which Manchester United had just beaten, announced through its president that it intended to propose that Manchester United should be declared the honorary European champions for the year.

Footballers who survived the crash included B. Foulkes, H. Gregg, Ray Wood, K. Morgans and Bobby Charlton.

Six hours after the crash a team of German investigators examined the wreckage of the Elizabethan under the glare of arc lights. Their initial statements as to the cause of the accident left no doubt that they held the actions, or inactions, of Captain Thain to be responsible. Beneath three inches of snow that had accumulated over the wings, prior to their arrival at the scene, they observed half an inch of rough ice that was bonded to the metal. They concluded that the ice had been present since the Elizabethan had first taxied out from the ramp. Furthermore this ice, by destroying the aerodynamic shape of the wings, had a detrimental effect on acceleration and increased the required take-off speed. They dismissed slush as a cause of the accident. Sixteen other aircraft that had taken off that day had all been deiced.

Just over a year passed before the German report was published. The accident was attributed to wing icing. The amount of slush present on the runway would only have increased the required take-off distance by 360 feet. Appended to their report was Thain's statement claiming that the slush affected the free running of the wheels. He believed that the ice observed on the wings had formed during the six hours before the investigators reached the scene. Publication of the German Report was followed by the despatch of a letter to Thain from the British Ministry of Civil Aviation. He was asked to show cause why his pilot's licence should not be revoked. Since the accident he had been suspended from flying duties by B.E.A. in accordance with the usual practice.

The flat rejection by the German authorities of any part that slush could have played was greeted with disbelief by pilots' associations and other interested organisations. In June 1959 Harold Watkinson, Minister for Civil Aviation, appointed a Commission to consider Thain's representations. This was the first time that a British tribunal was asked to review an accident that had already been investigated by a foreign authority. The members of the Commission were Mr E.S. Fay Q.C., Professor A. Collar, who had scientific qualifications, and an airline pilot, Captain R.P. Wigley.

They were asked to answer three questions: (1) Had Thain taken sufficient steps to satisfy himself that his wings were free of ice and snow? (2) Was the runway fit to use? (3) Did the difficulties encountered on the first two attempts to take-off justify a third attempt?

Even before the Fay Commission was ready to reply the German authorities declared that there was absolutely no just-ification for a new enquiry.

The Fay Commission issued its Report in August 1960. They acknowledged that Thain had observed water running off the trailing-edge and that the station engineer, standing on the wing during refuelling, observed no ice. But 78 minutes had passed since refuelling had taken place when the aircraft had left the ramp for the third time. Thain should then have made a personal inspection of the wings before deciding either to have them swept or deiced.

Regarding the condition of the runway, Thain had seen it being used by arriving and departing aircraft without any complaints being received from the pilots. He had no reason to suspect that the runway length would be insufficient. In making the third attempt to take off he had acted correctly after the station engineer had diagnosed the trouble. The Commission made it clear that they did not accept that ice on the wings had caused the accident. Professor Collar demonstrated that tests proved that drag caused by slush increased as the aircraft speed increased. The Commission had interviewed three persons who had taken part in rescue operations after the crash; they had not observed any ice on the wings. In any case freezing at 0°C or even slightly below is an extremely slow process.

They had also taken evidence from two Air Traffic Controllers who had watched the final attempt to take off. Both agreed that it began normally. After the nosewheel had been raised it touched down again some seconds later, then again left the ground before the aircraft overshot the runway. The Commission attributed this to the Elizabethan running into deeper slush or frozen slush.

The British Air Line Pilots' Association welcomed the Report of the Fay Commission as a clear indication that the true cause of the accident had not been established. Further research should be undertaken. The Ministry of Civil Aviation notified Thain that he could re-qualify for his pilot's licence if he reapplied. But the latter's professional future remained bleak. He received a notice of dismissal from B.E.A. for failing to have ordered the upper surface of the wings to be swept or deiced. In addition he had broken B.E.A.'s rules by allowing his co-pilot to occupy the left-hand seat.

In January 1961 his appeal against dismissal was rejected. Airlines have always been reluctant to employ pilots after they have been involved in accidents that have attracted unfavourable publicity. The Fay Commission had not blamed Thain for the accident, although he had been criticised over the failure to have the wings swept. But the death and injury of so many of those on board had put the pilot's name in the spotlight. If he had been re-employed many of his passengers would suffer a nervous reaction when the identity of their captain was broadcast.

B.E.A. anticipated claims from the relatives of those killed and injured, particularly if negligence was proven. They consulted Professor A.D. Young, Head of the Department of Aeronautical Engineering at London University; it was his opinion that slush was probably the only cause of the accident. Manchester United engaged Professor Owen, Professor of Fluid Mechanics at the University of Manchester; he refuted the German contention that slush drag decreased with speed – it *increased* with speed. He thought it highly probable that the accident was entirely due to slush.

In January 1963, after the Germans had again refused to reopen the enquiry, the Royal Aircraft Establishment at Farnborough (R.A.E.) conducted experiments using an Elizabethan. Taking part were Mr E.C. Markell, their Senior Principal Scientific Officer and Mr R. Szukiewicz, aerodynamicist of Hawker Siddeley Aviation. They found that 1/4 of an inch of slush would apply such braking effect that 50% more runway would be required than on a dry runway. Therefore on that day in Munich 7,500 feet would be needed. The airport's runway was only 6,600 feet in length. Agreeing that the accident could be explained by the presence of slush alone they also considered the effect of icing on the wings. They published tables to cover a varying thickness of ice. If 5 millimetres had covered 45% of the wings the increase of take-off speed required would not exceed three knots.

In November 1965 the Germans finally reopened the enquiry. Their report, published in August 1966, obstinately maintained, in the face of all the new evidence, that wing icing had been the essential cause for the accident: slush was an added one. In Britain tests continued on the effects both of slush and the propensity of aircraft to aquaplane on water. New deductions were published that year and in subsequent years.

How helpful was all of this to the unfortunate Captain James Thain? He had been vindicated but his career had not merely been interrupted: it had ended. He had occupied himself in poultry farming and was only 54 years of age when he died in August 1975. It would not be untrue to declare him to be the 24th victim of the Munich air disaster.

CONCLUSION

The last fifty years have witnessed a huge improvement in the construction of aircraft, their engines and equipment. Storm-warning radar has made it possible to avoid the worst areas of bad weather. Modern altimeters present an unambiguous reading. Instrument landing systems allow pilots to make approaches on runways in conditions of low cloud and poor visibility. Not every airport in the world is adequately equipped but responsible airlines are jealous of their reputation for safe operating standards.

In 1957 the introduction by B.O.A.C. of Bristol Britannias coincided with the first use of flight simulators. These allow instructors to observe the reactions of trainees to failures of one or more instruments, systems or engines. By 1965 the flight recorder, known to the general public as the "Black Box," monitored five parameters; these were the indicated airspeed, indicated altitude, magnetic heading, vertical acceleration and pitch attitude. Ten years later legislation required 26 parameters to be recorded.

The accident to a Trident airliner minutes after take-off from London Airport in 1972 resulted in legislation requiring the installation of a cockpit voice recorder. The flight recorder had revealed that, 114 seconds after take-off, the airliner had been flying well below the recommended speed. Someone then selected the droop lever up. Two seconds later the automatic stick shaker operated to warn the pilot of an imminent stall. Someone in the cockpit disconnected the stall recovery system and the Trident crashed, killing all 188 persons on board.

One sequel to this tragic event was the inclusion in the Trident flight simulator programme of the consequences when the flaps or droops were selected up too soon or when the aircraft was flying too slowly.

Today flying is generally perceived to be statistically safer than motor transport. The travelling public clearly recognises this and is not deterred from flying in a twin-engined airliner across the Atlantic ocean.

Inevitably there will continue to be accidents the cause of which cannot swiftly or easily be explained. Nevertheless the Civil Aviation Authority rates the chance of being involved in a fatal accident on a U.K.-registered aircraft as one in ten million.